QUESTIONS YOU SHOULD ASK
ABOUT CHARTER SCHOOLS
AND VOUCHERS

QUESTIONS YOU SHOULD ASK ABOUT CHARTER SCHOOLS AND VOUCHERS

Seymour B. Sarason
Yale University

HEINEMANN
Portsmouth, NH

As usual, I thank God that Lisa Pagliaro could read my handwriting.

Heinemann
A division of Reed Elsevier Inc.
361 Hanover Street
Portsmouth, NH 03801–3912
www.heinemann.com

Offices and agents throughout the world

The author and publisher wish to thank those who have generously given permission to reprint borrowed material:

Excerpts from *Going It Alone: A Study of Massachusetts Charter Schools* (Abbey Weiss, 1997) are used by permission of the Institute for Responsive Education, Northeastern University, Boston, MA.

Library of Congress Cataloging-in-Publication Data
Sarason, Seymour Bernard, 1919-
   Questions you should ask about charter schools and vouchers / Seymour B. Sarason.
       p. cm.
   Includes bibliographical references.
   ISBN 0-325-00405-6 (alk. paper)
      1. Charter schools—United States. 2. Educational vouchers—United States. 3. School choice—United States. I. Title.

LB2806.36 .S275 2002
379.1'11'0973—dc21   2001051603

Editor: Lois Bridges
Production editor: Sonja S. Chapman
Cover design: Catherine Hawkes, Cat & Mouse
Cover photo: © Jana Leon, Photonica
Typesetter: Argosy
Manufacturing: Steve Bernier

Printed in the United States of America on acid-free paper
06   05   04   03   02   VP   1   2   3   4   5

To Dr. Irma Miller
About whom I have no questions

CONTENTS

PREFACE

On the level of theory, research, policy, and action, the public schools have always been a source of controversy. The substance of the debates would erupt at least once every decade depending on significant issues the country was confronting. Immigration, the economy, juvenile crime, and religion were the most frequent issues. After and largely because of the social dynamics unleashed by World War II, controversy about public education slowly but steadily, at first, and then with increased speed came to be continuous front-page fare. If you had to pick a date when that speed mightily accelerated, you would be justified in choosing the day in 1954 when the Supreme Court rendered its unanimous desegregation decision. Prior to President Reagan, in no presidential campaign was education a major issue. In every campaign since, including his initial one, education has been a major issue of debate. There are two assertions about which everyone appears to be in complete agreement, however dramatically they differ in other respects. The first is that our schools are not accomplishing their intellectual and academic mission, especially in regard to urban students. The second is that unless schools are improved, the social and economic health of our society will continue to go downhill.

What has enabled science to contribute mightily to the store of human knowledge? There are many reasons, but for my present purposes three are most relevant. The first is that scientists came to take for granted that the more you know the more you need to know: problem creation through problem solution. The second reason, related to the first, is that things are never as simple as appearances suggest or we would like them to be; the human mind is our greatest ally and foe: Our capacity to misinterpret, ignore, and oversimplify is deep. The last reason is that science has a built-in morality which has a self-correcting function: You provide your peers, regardless of where they are in the world, with what you experienced and found in a way that is sufficiently complete and replicable. In the case of efforts for educational reform, these three reasons are hardly manifested. For example, reform efforts are not written up in anything resembling even a semi-complete fashion. This is not to say they are devoid of importance and should be relegated to the dustbin of history, since they may be of interest and instruction to those who will till similar soil. But none of them addresses a number of questions. Why and by whom were you given permission to carry out the reform? Were those who were the objects of reform—and they are always teachers—participants in the decision to go ahead? And if they were not, as is usually the case, what problems did you encounter that interfered in small and large ways with what you sought to accomplish? How did you deal with the issues and with what degree of success? What problems did you encounter that you did not or could not predict? If you had to do it over again, would you do it differently and why? What did you learn about yourself, your ideas, and the limitations imposed on efforts of non-cosmetic reform?

Over nearly a half century I have observed many reform efforts and have come to know rather well a fair number of reformers. The reader is undoubtedly familiar with Murphy's law regarding doctoral dissertations: If anything can go wrong, it will. In the case of reform efforts I have proposed Sarason's law: Murphy's law is a gross underestimation. That was my experience and to a person I have never known a reformer who said that my law was not totally valid. What they and I learned the hard way is that schools (and school systems) are fantastically complicated institutions whose traditions, personnel, and culture are deeply intractable to change. Schools are not unique institutions; they are just different, but it is a huge difference in terms of the lives of millions of students and parents, as well as of the society. Educational reformers knew this before they initiated their reforms but they knew it in the abstract, in a very superficial way. But when it is all over, they know it in a way that will ever be with them. But *how* and *why* they acquired this knowledge about the culture of the school is not in their write-ups. It therefore serves no self-correcting influence on others who will make similar efforts, and it also blinds people generally to the culture of the school in which reforms are initiated.

When an anthropologist plans to experience and study a culture foreign to him, he is obliged to read what is available about that culture. Even so, when he arrives there he seeks to find an informant who by virtue of status, personality, or whatever can tell him who can be trusted to tell which individuals can provide the information relevant to the questions for which he seeks answers. It does not take the anthropologist more than a couple of weeks to learn that despite all he has read and the colleagues he has consulted, the culture is puzzling and strange and obviously more complex and inscrutable than he had imagined.

In the chapters that follow, what I have said in this preface is relevant to the two currently much discussed educational reforms: charter schools and vouchers. This is not to say that I discuss them in a comprehensive way. The issues are many and thorny and I have restricted myself to several major facets that will serve as an introduction to and an appreciation of the complexities these reforms present us. There is a lot at stake. We can ill afford more well-intentioned reforms for which we end up with a very insecure basis for assessing their claims. It is not only a matter of analyzing numerical data, about which I will say little, but about being able to say why the reform works in one site and does not in another site. It is only when we have gained that level of comprehension that improving the reform becomes possible. For improvement to take place requires that we seek answers to important questions to which the history of educational reform has sensitized us.

CHAPTER 1

THE PURPOSES OF THIS BOOK

This book is for those people who, for whatever reasons, have not had cause to familiarize themselves with the major issues charter schools and vouchers pose. I have no doubt that these people have heard about the two movements and may even have taken pro or con positions about them. However, my experience in talking with them (educators, parents, political officialdom) forced me to conclude that they are vastly over-simplifying a very complicated set of issues. That is not sur-prising, and for two reasons. First, charter schools and vouch-ers are relatively new phenomena on the educational scene. Second, the proponents and opponents have articulated their positions with understandable passion and conviction pre-cisely because they see each other as adversaries and in the process publicize their positions in brief, simplistic ways. They take part in the quest to shape public opinion and polit-ical action. That is why I accepted the invitation to write a modest-sized book in which I could discuss some of the major issues which any concerned, literate adult should take into account when thinking about and discussing charter schools and vouchers. The issues are complicated but they are not mysteries. But I must warn the reader that complexities can only be sensed or recognized if the reader can perform the difficult act of suspending whatever judgments she has already made about charter schools and vouchers. That is ask-ing a lot of the reader, and I say that because I personally found it hard to do. In principle I have been in favor of char-ter schools and vouchers, but the ways in which they have been conceived and implemented have forced me to conclude that it is highly unlikely we will ever have a secure evidential basis for judging their outcomes. And that is the major point in this book. We have had a surfeit of educational reforms and in almost all instances we have ended up not knowing what and how much to believe about their claims. Will it be any different with charter schools and vouchers? Will they be two more instances where potentially fruitful ideas will have similar fates?

By asking those questions I am saying to proponents and opponents that charter schools and vouchers have to be seen in terms of the limitations of past reforms. Granted that vouchers and charter schools are different from past reforms, the fact remains that we are obligated to require that there is or will be a basis for judgment that goes beyond personal opinion or anecdote. That is a requirement that opponents of charter schools have totally ignored; their opposition has been unreflective, emotional, and a reflection of a vested interest. It is a requirement that proponents have also totally ignored, confusing expectations with accomplished fact. I am not pronouncing a "plague on both your houses." I am suggesting to both that there is a way of proceeding from which we can learn what we need to learn. If after reading this book you agree with me that the issues are more complicated than you thought, I will be more than satisfied. I do not expect total agreement. I know the difference between the lures of fantasy and the brute force of experienced realities, an inequality that makes a very big difference in how we approach the future.

I have written a good deal about charter schools and past educational reforms. Putting what I have learned in a very condensed form has not been easy. I have avoided some issues of a conceptual, methodological, analytical-statistical nature with which, however important, I did not want to burden the reader, who, I assume, needs or wishes an introduction to the ins and outs of the charter school and voucher movements. It is this kind of audience I have sought to reach. For readers who may be curious about where I am coming from, the bibliography includes some of my writings to which I have not made direct reference in these pages but which, at the least, indicate that I have observed, participated in, and written about educational reform for over four decades. As I have emphasized in the last chapter of this book, charter schools and vouchers, like all other reform efforts, obligate everyone to ask and answer the most important question of all: What is the most important purpose of schooling, which if not realized makes the realization of all other purposes very problematic? It is easy to ask that question; it is not easy for people to answer it other than with vague generalizations. Neither opponents nor proponents have asked that question or even hinted at anything resembling a concrete answer. I have no doubt that future historians of education will be puzzled about why that question was for all practical purposes treated, when it was treated at all, so superficially.

Charter schools and vouchers have been discussed with far more heat than illumination. Charter school reform was first initiated in 1991 in Minnesota and over the next ten years many other states followed suit. At present there are upward of three thousand charter schools. The fact is that we as yet have very little data by which to pass judgment on them. And by data I mean findings which would stand up in a court of evidence. In short, proponents and opponents cannot as yet say that their claims are justified. In the case of school choice, which permits parents to place their children in the school of their choice in their local school district, a policy many districts have adopted in the past decade, we again have little data (really no data) by which to judge the efficacy of the policy. As for vouchers, which in principle give parents a clearly stated sum to be used to send their children to the private or parochial school of their choice, there are perhaps two or three communities which have adopted that policy on a very modest basis. For all practical purposes we again have little basis for passing judgment.

The reader may ask: If there is little or no evidence which allows us to pass judgment, pro or con, is not your book premature? One part of my answer is that a surprising number of school personnel (teachers and administrators) have not had the opportunity or stimulation to become knowledgeable about the rationale for these reforms and tend almost instinctively to react negatively to them. They make the same mistake as the proponents who think that what they are advocating contains the answer to our educational problems and, thereby, grossly oversimplify the issues involved. Someone once said that it is hard to be completely wrong, but in the case of these reforms that is precisely what opponents say about proponents, and vice versa. That black-white stance has always been a feature of educational reform, which in part explains why educational reform has such a sorry, troubled history. The other and related part of my answer is addressed to those with little knowledge of the many past reform efforts in the post–World War II era. Although I shall have little to say about that past, it is my hope that I can alert the reader to the questions and issues that are relevant to any educational reform effort even though on the surface the reforms I shall discuss seem so different from past efforts. They are different, but not in terms of how educational policy is conceived, adopted, implemented, and evaluated. And they certainly are identical in one obviously crucial respect: They seek to influence, alter, and improve a public institution considered not to be achieving its purposes. Every reform rests on a diagnosis of why schools fall far short of their mark. Each rests on a conception of what I call the culture of the school—more correctly, the culture of school systems: their structure, layers of administration, age grading, behavioral and programmatic regularities, undergirding assumptions about the nature and contexts of learning and about the "psychology" of the intellectual and social development of young people. One is justified in concluding that any non-cosmetic reform is taking aim at a very complex institution which has changed surprisingly little in its cultural-social-organizational features. If the educational reforms in the post World War II era have been disappointing, can it be that the reformers have failed to focus on one feature of the culture of schools—or have misjudged its consequences—that is of paramount importance in explaining why reforms have been so ineffective? The proponents of charter schools, school choice, and vouchers have raised and answered that question. Their answer can be put most briefly at this point in our discussion by two words: power relationships. Put in another way, these proponents rivet on issues of power they consider inimical to change, innovation, and improvement. Charter schools and vouchers are the most radical challenges ever to how power is allocated and used within the school system and between the school system and the community in which it is embedded. In that sense charter schools and vouchers are explicitly revolutionary. In one instance new power is given to parents, and in the other power is given to a school to be "free" of any existing school system. It should not be surprising that these two reforms arouse passionate controversy. So, although we are not in the position to say that these two reforms are or are not achieving their purposes, we should feel *professionally* obligated to judge their rationales as fairly and objectively as possible.

It is not enough to oppose a reform because it is new, challenging, and upsetting to the status quo, reactions understandable from school personnel who indeed have a vested interest in schools as they have known them. Similarly, proponents of these reforms should not blithely assume that the objections of school personnel have no merit whatsoever and that they are mindlessly opposed to school reform. There is a difference between discussing issues and criticizing personalities by attaching pejorative labels to them, and that distinction has determined what I say in the following pages. This book is about issues and the questions to be directed to those who take different positions about them.

In a book by intention clearly limited in length, it is not possible to discuss all issues at length. As I said at the outset, we have as yet no credible, let alone compelling, basis for making final judgments. But when those data begin to be made public, we should be prepared to scrutinize and judge them in order to determine whether they contain answers to questions we have previously thought about. That is why I do not think this book is premature.

In the following chapter I shall have more to say about a particular issue that, far from being premature, gets to the core of how one judges the predicted success of new, untried educational reforms like charter schools and vouchers. It should force one to adapt a "show me" stance. The issue is not whether a reform should be given a chance to demonstrate its claims but rather whether it is being done in a way that will provide us clear, compelling data for making a judgment. For example, the New York State Board of Regents instituted changes affecting almost three million schoolchildren. Graduation standards were raised, tests given to ensure those standards are met, and districts informed that they had to close the achievement gap between rich and poor children. This has met with opposition from some of the state's better schools. In an editorial in the May 14, 2001, edition of the *New York Times*, the following is said (the italics are mine):

> Some local school officials have asked to be exempted from state tests on the grounds that the new tests are forcing them to "dumb down" already excellent curriculums. But the Regents should not accept claims of excellence on *faith*. Districts must demonstrate their accomplishments in *verifiable* ways that allow the state to draw comparisons across districts as well as racial and ethnic groups.
>
> Schools that wish to avoid the state tests can always appeal to the State Education Department's alternative assessment panel, which allows select schools to deviate from the standard assessment package if the alternatives are *rigorous* and include *valid* techniques for evaluating student performance. This is a reasonable exemption that allows the preservation of high standards across the state. The Legislature should resist further pressure to replace statewide standards with a balkanized system of locally defined standards that would make it impossible to compare educational quality from one community or school to another.

How can you be against a stance that disqualifies faith and personal opinion as a basis of judgment and calls for what I call credible data, meaning that those data will pass muster in a court of evidence? But what the editorial says nothing about is that the data it seeks requires schools to have personnel who have the technical sophistication to obtain and analyze data uncontaminated by personal bias, and to draw conclusions justified by the rules of evidence and logic and superior to alternative conclusions critics of the reform could advance. If the history of science has taught anything, it is that the human mind is our greatest ally and foe; it can come up with brilliant ideas but it also can ignore the sources of error our ideas contain. It took a millennium for people to take seriously that certain findings and phenomena were inexplicable by the assumption that Earth was the center of the universe. And when they questioned it they were punished as heretics who were calling into question religious explanations which, as an act of faith, were considered "self-evidently true." When the editorial uses such terms as "rigorous" and "variable," it is raising the question of scientific evidence at the same time it totally ignores the fact that schools have neither the personnel, the time, nor the funds to do "evaluations" which tell us whether the claims of reform advocates should be taken seriously. I know of no school system that has in its budget funds for serious evaluation. I am not suggesting that schools should be research laboratories. I am saying something more practical and applied as well as socially, institutionally, and morally responsible: Schools should be obliged to give us persuasive data relevant to the accomplishment of their stated purposes. That they are now not so obliged is not the fault of schools. Society has not mandated such an obligation, let alone funded it.

The imagery most people have about schools is woefully incomplete and misleading. Schools, let alone school systems, are very complicated places in terms of organization and structure; how their personnel are selected and by whom; variations in classroom ambiance; the quality of interpersonal relations; range in age and pedagogy of teachers; quality and quantity of school-parent contacts; sources of formal and informal power; decision-making processes; modes of surfacing and dealing with teacher-student, teacher-parent, teacher-principal, and teacher-teacher conflicts; school-community relationships; and much more. I have discussed this in all of my writings, especially my 1996 book, *Revisiting the Culture of the School and the Problem of Change.* And what I have described becomes most clear when the school is pressured to change, when its accustomed way of doing things is challenged. It is then that the complicated culture of the school hits you, so to speak, in the face. Underestimating that complexity goes a long way in explaining why educational reform has been so ineffective. It follows, therefore, that evaluating a reform is the opposite of simple.

What I have just said is no less true for a charter school. Indeed, it is more complicated than a regular school because it is being created by people who have never had the experience of creating a school intended to be different from those in which they had previously worked. That is a difference that makes a big difference. You would think that precisely because they are a new type of school and much is expected of them that charter school legislation would include funds for a serious evaluation. But I know of no state that included such a provision and, as a result, it is most unlikely—I would say totally unlikely—that we will be in the position to explain how this charter school fell far short of the mark and why that one claims success. And these words are being written by someone who in principle is favorable to the concepts of charter schools.

By what criteria will we judge charter schools? That is the first question, an obvious one. The second question is the one that gets ignored: By what kinds of data will we understand why and to what degree charter schools and their claims will stand up in the court of evidence? Those are questions we can ask now, even before we possess data relevant to their answers. That is why in the next chapter I will illustrate the significance of these questions by reviewing some past reforms for which we know the outcomes. On the surface these reforms are unrelated to vouchers and charter schools, but in terms of the two major questions I stated above they are, so to speak, kissing cousins. It is not a happy story, but that is the point: Those questions never received the scrutiny they deserved. And that is what appears to be the case in regard to charter schools and vouchers.

CHAPTER 2

WHY WE SHOULD SUSPEND JUDGMENT

There are several reasons school personnel should have more than superficial knowledge of the charter school and voucher movements. The word *movements* is important because unlike most proposals for educational reform, which far more often than not go nowhere on the level of action, charter schools and vouchers are being taken seriously and are being implemented. The same is less the case for vouchers but there is good reason to believe that it is picking up steam and support from political leaders and wealthy private-sector individuals providing large sums of money to families dissatisfied with their children's schools but financially unable to send them to private or parochial schools. In the past several presidential campaigns charter schools and vouchers were hotly discussed. Indeed, President George W. Bush made it crystal clear that he was in favor of charter schools and vouchers and his election signals that he and his supporters will invigorate further the two movements. It would be folly for school personnel to assume that these two movements will fade away in the foreseeable future.

Opponents and proponents of charter schools and vouchers agree on one thing: Our schools are not accomplishing their educational mission. However they differ in their explanations for this state of affairs, they agree that educational reform, like reforming and strengthening Medicare and the Social Security system, should be at the top of the national agenda. That point cannot be overemphasized because it reflects a degree of disappointment, among people generally, far greater than ever before in our national history. That should not be surprising to school personnel but it is. After all, in the post–World War II era *billions upon billions upon billions* have been expended to improve schools with little to show for it. Indeed, whereas in earlier decades school personnel enjoyed a high degree of public respect and support, that is not the case today. That explains, in part at least, why a few years after becoming a teacher, many teachers leave the field or retire as early as they can, or say that they would dissuade their children from seeking a career in teaching. Respect for and recognition of what one does is what we all need and want and when these are not experienced, it is hard to persist. For example, why is it that not until the sixties did the teacher unions begin to grow in size and militancy? By far the most frequent answer has been that teacher salaries were so immorally and scandalously low, and community support for increases so weak and begrudging, that teachers felt compelled to join the unions; what they could not accomplish as individuals they could as an organized force. That is a valid answer but it obscures the fact that what teachers did day in and day out was accorded neither respect nor recognition.

In subsequent years the respect and recognition factors emerged in a different societal context. As it became clear with each passing year that educational outcomes were getting poorer rather than improving, criticisms of school personnel became louder and clearer, and from different sources ranging from the university to minority groups. It was as if our educational ills were created and sustained by school personnel. That school personnel played a role should not be surprising but to focus criticism largely on school personnel was the grossest of oversimplifications of a very complicated problem. It was Henry Mencken who said that for every important social problem there was a simple answer that was wrong. Blaming school personnel confirms his caveat. If the critics confirmed the caveat, it is also true that school personnel had a superficial understanding of how complicated the problem was and, therefore, in replying to the critics they could not put on the table for discussion questions that would expose how narrow and misleading the substance of the criticisms was. Proponents and opponents lived in and experienced different worlds. They talked past each other. They appended different pejorative labels to each other. Recognition of the complexity of the problem—really an assortment of interrelated problems—was the victim.

Relatively speaking, charter schools and vouchers are recent developments and the battle lines have already been drawn. It is my hope that school personnel will not repeat the mistakes of the past, mistakes of omission, knowledge, and name calling. If those mistakes are not to be repeated, it will require that school personnel adopt a stance that may be difficult but absolutely necessary: Suspend whatever judgment, pro or con, you have about charter schools and vouchers and come along with me in exploring this question: What questions should we, must we, ask and answer in deciding when and if a serious non-cosmetic educational reform deserves to be spread and supported in as many schools as possible? Assume that advocates of these reforms have no nefarious motivations; they are well-intentioned individuals who want to improve schools. Saying that will inevitably remind you that the road to hell is paved with good intentions, but that, we should remember, is no less applicable to us.

There is another way I could put what I have asked the reader to try to do and that is to imagine that you have developed a plan and strategy to improve educational outcomes, and you are given the opportunity to appear before a funding committee, public or private, to tell them why they should provide you with funds to develop and spread your plan. What are the questions you should be prepared to answer? Keep in mind that the questions you will be asked are those which should be asked of any serious educational reform effort.

In order to give the reader some idea of the direction and substance of the discussion, it may be helpful if I very briefly discuss a federal agency charged with the responsibility of approving new drugs and medical technology before they can be marketed to and used by the medical community. I am referring to the Federal Drug Administration (FDA). Before there was an FDA, physicians and pharmaceutical companies could develop a drug and then market it. For all practical purposes they were free to develop and market whatever they wanted. There was no FDA to ask questions about the basis for claiming that the drug would have the desired effects claimed for it. What were its near-and long-term side effects? For what illnesses or diseases was the drug intended or claimed to be therapeutic? What evidence from pilot studies demonstrated clearly the degree of effectiveness of the drug? What evidence was there that these pilot studies were carried out in a careful, objective manner immune to the criticism of the role of personal opinion, insufficient descriptive detail, lack of clear and stringent criteria for selecting subjects for treatment, failure to demonstrate that experimental and control groups were comparable, that the negative side effects of the drug were too many and dangerous to justify approval, and more? To get approval is a long, expensive process justified by the agency's responsibility to protect the public, to assure the public that the drug is safe and effective; it does what it claims to do. The questions the FDA asks of every application for approval are many and clear. Many of those questions were sharpened and new ones added as experience revealed the inadequacies of past questions. The questions the FDA asks and the criteria it uses to judge the quality and quantity of the evidence it expects in the answers are critical. That expectation is rooted in two conclusions drawn from the historical record. The first is that the human mind is man's greatest ally and foe. We are capable of great achievements and an equally great capacity to deceive ourselves. The second is that there are rules about what constitutes credible, compelling evidence for the validity of your claims. That you think and feel that your ideas are valid is just that: *your* thinking and *your* feelings, in which you have a very personal stake. But if you want others to agree with and applaud you, you should be obligated to present *evidence* that in the "real world" your ideas work the way you say they do.

There is nothing remotely resembling the FDA in the educational community or in state and federal governments where charter school and voucher legislation originated as have past major and much-heralded reform efforts. It is second nature at the FDA to look at any application for approval with this question: How knowledgeable is the applicant about past efforts—their findings, errors of omission and commission—and how is the applicant going to take them into account? As we shall see in later chapters, the charter school and voucher movements have proceeded as if there is no theoretical, descriptive research literature relevant to their purpose, as if the history of the field is indeed bunk. We are frequently and correctly warned that to ignore history is to set the stage to repeat its mistakes, a caveat that explains a good deal about why educational reform has had so many failures. I do not expect school personnel to be avid readers of the history of educational reform, but I do expect that school personnel can and should, at the very least, ask of any reform effort: How is the way you are *conceiving* and *implementing* your reform avoiding the mistakes that have plagued past reform efforts? I italicize implementing because there have been many reform efforts whose purposes are necessary and laudable but whose mode of implementation has defeated those purposes. There is an irony here. If I do not expect school personnel to be knowledgeable about the history of reform, in later pages I will point out that by virtue of being in the school culture, school personnel know a good deal about the obstacles a reform will predictably encounter, obstacles reformers ignore or gloss over. When it comes to implementation they need not regard themselves as babes in the woods, as passive pawns in the arena of reform. (They, especially teachers, know that any reform for which they have had no input, or a perfunctory one, is in trouble before it gets off the ground.)

I initially intended that the next chapter would be devoted to charter schools. I changed my mind because I decided that it might be helpful to the reader briefly to describe and discuss a past reform effort which on the surface had nothing to do with charter schools or vouchers but below the surface had a good deal of relevance to the two movements. It is a sad but very instructive story. It would be a disservice to the reader to leave him or her with the impression that the questions we ask about charter schools and vouchers are unique to these reforms and, therefore, we have nothing to learn from past reform efforts. The fact is that past reform efforts have been disappointing because these questions were not taken seriously. Yes, charter schools and vouchers are different from past reforms but from the obligation to judge them the questions we must ask are identical in principle and purpose. As professionals and concerned citizens we have to adopt a questioning stance which increases the chances that we will learn from our mistakes and oversimplifications.

CHAPTER 3

LESSONS FROM PAST REFORMS

The following excerpt is from an article in *Education Week* in its September 25, 1991, issue.

Three years after the Annie E. Casey Foundation committed $50 million to an ambitious five-year effort to raise student achievement and stem dropout rates, teenage pregnancy, and youth unemployment in five cities, project participants' initial enthusiasm and optimism have been tempered by a healthy dose of reality.

"This was the first time we had a five-year commitment and a sense of quite a bit of money to work with to address youth issues comprehensively," recalled James Van Vleck, a retired Mead Corporation senior vice president and the chairman of the interagency collaborative overseeing the grant in Dayton, Ohio.

"It made us think it was going to be a piece of cake," he said.

But Casey Foundation executives and project leaders now admit that the "piece of cake" was much bigger and more difficult to digest than they had first imagined.

They recount story after story about how complicated it has been to coordinate the efforts of a wide range of youth-serving institutions, including schools and human-service agencies.

They talk about the difficulties of implementing change from the top down and of the price to be paid for not including educators fully in the process. And they tick off the problems that come with expecting results too quickly and now acknowledge that it will take much longer than originally anticipated to bring about lasting change.

"As we've sobered up and faced the issues," Mr. Van Vleck said, "we have found that getting collaboration between those players is a much more complicated and difficult game than we expected."

I confess that it is hard, really impossible, for me to react charitably to this report. It is easy to give brownie points for good intentions, but how do you grade an effort that managed to make every mistake predictable from similar past efforts? How should you react to an endeavor so ignorant of the cumulative wisdom gained from these past efforts? The Casey Foundation program exemplifies an attempt at primary prevention of certain problems that required *initially* the reform of the relationships within and among diverse agencies. Proclaiming the virtues and goals of primary prevention does not earn you a badge of honor when you are ignorant of what you need to accomplish for your objectives to be realized. Primary prevention does not avoid complexities; it brings them to the fore. To forget that, assuming you once knew it, is to be governed by a time perspective guaranteed to defeat you.

Apparently no one at the Casey Foundation saw the similarity in *principle* between their goals of primary prevention and those that powered the curriculum changes of the sixties. Let me illustrate by the new math which, if not heralded as a panacea, came uncomfortably close. The primary prevention goals of the new math were explicit and several: to prevent in students an aversion to math, to instill in them an enjoyment of math, to bring about a higher level of math skills and performance, and to increase the number of students desirous of pursuing a scientific career needed by a scientific-technological society. As a nation, we were told, we could not afford to let a bad situation become worse. We had to prevent in future generations what had happened to past ones (Sarason 1996).

The new math (as well as the new physics, new biology, new social studies), consistent with the rationale of primary prevention, was *not* geared to be helpful to individuals with existing problems in math; it was *not* a clinical or repair or rehabilitative effort. It was geared to influence the total population of students in ways that over time would discernibly decrease the incidence of untoward attitudes and deficits related to math. It is important to emphasize that primary prevention is not oriented to this or that *individual* but rather to a class of people within which, it is hoped, the incidence of a problem or condition will decrease. It is the difference between trying to get someone who smokes to give up the habit and trying to persuade people not to take up smoking. One could as well use obesity, drugs, and alcohol as examples.

The new math was a disaster. It is not being unfair to say it had iatrogenic consequences: It made a bad situation worse. The Casey Foundation had millions of dollars and good intentions. The new math advocates had a new curriculum and good intentions. The Casey Foundation was ignorant of the school and agency cultures. The new mathers were ignorant of the culture of schools, life in the modal classroom, the preparation of teachers, what was involved in helping teachers *unlearn* conventional ways of thinking and teaching, and the helplessness of parents for whom the new math was a foreign language.

If it is understandable that the Casey Foundation did not see kinship with the new math debacle, it is scandalous that they were unaware of President Nixon's Experimental Schools Program (ESP). That program not only had the support of the president but also that of the president's Science Advisory Committee and the top officials in the Department of Health, Education, and Welfare. The ESP was based explicitly on a recognition of the inadequacies of past efforts, a recognition that was as refreshing as it was singular. Very briefly, the ESP rested on several considerations:

• Past federal efforts to improve and change schools were largely failures.

• Federal programs had a buckshot quality: There was a program for this part of the school system and for that one; there was a program for this educational problem and for that one. It was as if the federal government kept reacting to whatever problem was brought to its attention. Sequence and interconnectedness were not important.

• The federal government should provide the resources for *comprehensive* change in a school system, that is, sufficient resources to permit a school district more meaningfully and efficiently "to pull it all together" in a single direction.

• There was merit in the complaints of local districts that federal imposition of programs, or too many intrusions by federal personnel into planning at the local level, robbed local people of initiative, creativity, and control. In the ESP, local people would have more control over ESP projects. If local districts were sincerely given the opportunity to change their schools in ways they considered most appropriate, one could then count on their commitment to initiate and sustain the change process.

• Federal efforts to evaluate past reform efforts had been inadequate and they bore no relationship either to changes in federal policy or to local program management. The ESP would use innovative and rigorous social science methodology to understand and assess the change process better. Indeed, somewhat less than one-third of the sixty to seventy million dollars that the ESP would cost would go to an evaluation scheme no less comprehensive than the changes that local districts would bring about in their schools.

The ESP was a disaster and anyone who has any doubts on that score should read Cowden and Cohen's (n.d.) federally sponsored assessment. Obviously, the Casey Foundation did not do so.

Most assuredly, I gain no satisfaction from having predicted the failure of the ESP, but one had to be inordinately obtuse not to have made such a prediction. Somewhere near the point when the policy makers were to decide which school districts would be part of the ESP, I was asked to come to Washington to advise on these decisions. It was a chaotic visit on several scores. Federal personnel felt tremendous pressure to launch the well-publicized program as soon as possible, preferably yesterday. I could not decide whether the pressure was more internal or external, although as the meeting wore on, the internal drive seemed to be the major source. That feeling of pressure seemed very much related to the federal personnel's vast underestimation of how much time it would take to select school districts. Because the local districts would have the most to say about how they would bring about comprehensive change, that kind of freedom made the task of selection very difficult. How does one choose on the basis of a written grant request (and telephone calls) except by resorting to one's own conception about how comprehensive change *should* be accomplished? That issue came quickly to the fore when one perused the written documents at different stages of their submission; they were vague statements of virtuous intent, giving one no sense of security about how "comprehensive change" was being defined. However committed federal personnel had been to the idea of local initiative and control, that commitment quickly began to dissolve as they concluded that local districts were defining comprehensive change in strange and various ways. The written documents were more like inkblots, forcing the reader to intuit what local districts meant by what they said and wrote. The truth is that the local districts were as much at sea about the meaning of "comprehensive change" as the federal personnel were.

My second contact with the ESP was a year later when I was asked to assess the plans and resources of a private consulting firm seeking the contract for the first in a series of evaluation studies. By this time most of the local districts to be part of the ESP had been chosen and their final grant applications were made available to us. Each application was no less than four inches thick and weighed five or more pounds. Their bulk was matched only by their lack of substance. That may sound like an excessively harsh judgment, but no one at this second meeting came to a contrary conclusion; it was obvious to everyone that these applications presented no focus to evaluate—no conceptual or procedural framework. It was painful to observe the staff of the consulting firm, a methodologically sophisticated group, trying to reconcile their desire to get the contract with the inkblot character of what they were supposed to do. The federal staff wanted a rigorous evaluation, but they had maneuvered themselves into a classically tragic situation in which the beginnings already contained the seeds of everyone's ultimate defeat. This judgment is well documented by Cowden and Cohen (n.d.) and will not be further discussed here.

I did not relate this and other experiences merely to indicate that initiating, managing, and sustaining comprehensive change involving schools and community agencies are complex affairs. Nor was it my intention to add to the collection of horror stories. My use of these instances was the basis they provided to make several points. The first is that any effort at primary prevention in schools, geared as it almost always is to the prevention of student problems, cannot ignore the necessity for the adults (professional or lay) who will implement the effort to change in ways consistent with that effort. Put another way, the effort always will require that these people literally reform their attitudes and practices. To put it more baldly: These people have to be seen initially as part of the problem, not as tailor-made for the solution. I am in no way suggesting that they should be viewed as clinical specimens possessing characteristics absent in "us." Like us, they come to the effort with attitudes and practices that contributed to the need for the new effort. To ignore this point, to proceed as if verbal agreement and commitment are sufficient for change, is defeating of one's goals.

That is why I said earlier that proclaiming adherence to the goals of primary prevention is not inherently virtuous. To achieve these goals requires processes and a long-term time perspective too frequently overlooked or egregiously oversimplified, which is another way of saying that your conception of the particular conditions you seek to prevent was woefully incomplete. The goals of primary prevention rest on some understanding of the factors contributing to the conditions you seek to prevent. In the case of our schools those conditions are *in part* always a reflection of the attitudes and practices of those who participate in the new effort.

The second, obviously related to the first, is that the goals of primary prevention are achievable only if the dynamics of secondary prevention have been successfully overcome. If those participating in the effort are *part* of the problem, how can you dilute the adverse consequences of their overlearned attitudes and practices? To get to the point where primary prevention becomes a possibility, you must have successfully confronted and overcome the consequences of these past attitudes and practices.

The third point is less obvious than the first two. Is it not a fateful mistake to formulate the goals of primary prevention *only* in terms of what you want to prevent in pupils? If it is indeed true that educational personnel are part of the problem, should we not be paying more attention to how we might select and prepare these personnel so that they will be less of a problem than they are now? Can our colleges of education better prepare personnel so as to make the achievement of primary prevention goals less messy, less of a failure than such efforts have been in the past?

What is it you want to prevent? That question has been almost always answered in terms of students. But if anything is clear from the history of educational reform—and anyone who has attempted any degree of educational change will attest to this—it is that what you want to prevent in students depends on the "reforming" of existing personnel and that is a task we do not do well. If we looked anew at the selection

22

and preparation of educational personnel from a primary prevention perspective—informed as that should be by the
cumulative wisdom attained from the failures of school
reform—might not that be productive? Is not such a perspective long overdue?

Schools of education have never been without their critics.
The most frequent and damning criticisms have been that
those seeking careers in education are intellectually of
mediocre quality, they are inadequately steeped in subject
matter and/or they are steeped in stultifying pedagogical
methodologies, and in the classroom they are unimaginative,
conforming, and unstimulating. If you had to summarize the
thrust of these criticisms, it would be that educational personnel are not the intellectuals their critics are. There is a kernel
of truth in these criticisms, but only a kernel. I shall have more
to say about this in later chapters. At this point in our discussion I wish only to indicate that examining the selection and
preparation of educational personnel from a primary prevention perspective is long overdue. If we could start from scratch
and design programs to prepare educational personnel—taking into account what we have experienced and learned about
the difficulties of changing attitudes and practices of those
personnel once they are in schools and socialized into the culture of schools—would we not do a better job of preventing
problems in students *and* educators, and would we not make
the task of implementing and sustaining reform in schools less
of a minefield of explosive failures? In my fifty years of experience in and around schools and educators I have heard only
a handful of people say that their preparation was adequate for
the realities of classrooms and schools. Apart from criticism of
educators by others, educators are, generally speaking, very
realistic critics of their professional training.

The past failures of educational reforms have brought in
their wake the conclusion that the problem is not in a primary
sense a financial one but a lack of knowledge about what will
work. Here, too, there is a kernel of truth but one that has
been dangerously and wrongly misused. When in the past I

23

have expressed a similar conclusion, it was always from the standpoint that reform efforts reflected diagnoses and conceptions guaranteed to be ineffective, and to proceed as if increasing expenditures would be fruitful was an invitation to disillusionment. This conclusion in no way implied that if we altered our view of things, money would not be a problem. Rather than lacking knowledge, we had gained a degree of cumulative wisdom that ought to be taken seriously. To argue, as did former Secretary of Education Alexander, that increased expenditures were not justified by existing knowledge speaks volumes about what he and his advisors do not know about what has been learned. Let us take Head Start as an illustrative case.

Head Start was powered by a diagnosis as correct as it was unverbalized. It was a program, the first, to take primary prevention seriously. If disadvantaged children were given an appropriate preschool experience, as children from more affluent backgrounds received, there would be a reduction in that group's incidence of school failure and low academic achievement. The diagnosis had several parts. The first was that these children were intellectually capable of normal educational achievement. Why, then, did so many of them not achieve once they started school? The second part of the diagnosis was that there was something in their backgrounds (familial, cultural) that was either "missing" or ill suited for school learning; that is, the "problem" was in these factors, not in the children. What went unverbalized was the clear implication that schools were and had long been ill suited for these children: *Schools* were a problem. The third part, also unverbalized, was based on a theory of "contagion": When these children entered school they caught the virus of disinterest, low motivation, and alienation. Head Start was to be a form of *inoculation* against catching the virus.

What has been the result? No one claims that Head Start has been a dramatic success, but on the basis of available evidence no one can claim that it has been a failure. That evidence indicates that there has been some decrease in the incidence of school failure or academic retardation. However, if one takes seriously the unverbalized contagion part of the original diagnosis—a part which is no less applicable to many so-called advantaged children—one has to ask why the inoculation should have been expected to have truly dramatic results. You could justifiably argue that if the culture of schools was part of the *problem* and not the *solution*, then the results of Head Start are indeed dramatic, that there was and is a "ceiling effect" imposed by the culture of schools, limiting what Head Start could accomplish—an effect against which any inoculation could be only *partially* effective. For too many students, advantaged or disadvantaged, schools are uninteresting, unstimulating places.

Now let us return to Secretary Alexander, who, on the *MacNeil/Lehrer Newshour* on October 2, 1991, stated that before the government increased expenditures for new educational reform efforts, we needed to have more secure knowledge about what works. To this Jonathan Kozol, also on the panel that night, asked, Since there was evidence that Head Start enjoyed some success—a conclusion the secretary had agreed with on that and previous occasions—why was it that there were no programs for the *majority* of children eligible for Head Start? The secretary was momentarily nonplussed and then spoke about the funding limitations imposed by the then-current recession, a reply that did not, of course, explain why in the more affluent eighties the same situation obtained.

We do not lack knowledge about the fruitfulness of primary prevention efforts in regard to education. I do not want to overevaluate what we know but neither do I want to ignore the ignorance belied by statements from officialdom. I think we know more about how to prevent problems than how to "solve" them once they have appeared. It is understandable that, faced with pressing, complicated, socially unsettling problems in education, people seek ways of repairing them. And it is understandable if they want near-term solutions. When you are, so to speak, on the firing line, the long-term view seems neither practical nor attractive. Nevertheless, the

25

imbalance between the support and encouragement of repair and primary preventive efforts is inexcusable, costly, and ultimately self-defeating.

As I said earlier, although the examples I have discussed were not about charter schools and vouchers, they illustrate issues that will be seen as directly relevant to how you should think about and judge those movements. That they are relevant should not be surprising, and for several reasons. I would say for obvious reasons. They each identify a school problem they wish to prevent and/or repair. They plan and come up with a strategy, time perspective, and the resources they think will be realistic, necessary, and effective. They know that to achieve their purposes will require that people will have to change their accustomed thinking and practices to a significant degree. They assume they know the culture of schools: its traditions, organizational features and dynamics, sources of conflict, decision-making processes, allocation of power, and response to criticism from external and internal sources. If they know all that, why, then, were their outcomes minimal or nonexistent? What errors of omission and commission, what knowledge of the experience of reformers of the past, were they not using? We can ask many other questions about the way the reformers were thinking and that is the point: We end up with questions and conclude that the reformers failed to ask themselves those questions, not the least important of which is, Are we oversimplifying the problem as many others have done in the past? Are we, like so many in the past, vastly underestimating that when you ask people to change their accustomed ways, you are asking a great deal of them, far more than you realize?

Let us turn to charter schools. I should tell the reader that although in principle I support the concept of charter schools, I have to predict that here again they will fall far short of their mark and for reasons I have briefly discussed in this chapter.

26

CHAPTER 4

CHARTER SCHOOLS:
AN ALTERNATIVE RATIONALE
FOR IMPLEMENTATION

I have asked the reader to suspend whatever judgments he or she may have, pro or con, about charter schools. That, I know, will be difficult to do. It was difficult for me, who in principle was favorable to the concept of charter schools. I hoped charter schools would serve the purposes of their creators to demonstrate that there was a credible alternative to schools as they are. That hope was based on a conclusion arrived at by many people, including countless schoolteachers and administrators, especially those in urban areas, although a significant number of school personnel in suburban middle and high schools also articulated that conclusion. The conclusion was that reforming schools was and would be futile. One teacher put well the gist of what other school personnel said less forthrightly: "I have heard all of the rhetoric about how schools must change. I have heard it from the different superintendents we have had here over the years. Nothing really changes, only the words, faces, and labels." It was a conclusion I and many people came to before charter schools came on the educational scene. When they did come onto the scene, school personnel reacted, initially at least, in two ways. One reaction was for all practical purposes no particular reaction at all, what you might call a "this too shall pass" reaction. Indeed, many school personnel could not tell me what the distinguishing features of charter schools were. That reaction began to change when the leadership of two major teacher unions took a stance very much opposed to charter school legislation. Their opposition was based on several arguments. First, it was another criticism of and an assault on the competence of school personnel and their resistance to innovation and change. Second, the cost of charter schools would reduce the funds available to underfinanced existing school systems. Third, charter schools would not have to deal with as heterogeneous a population of students as public schools were obliged to educate. These arguments were persuasive to many parents opposed to what they perceived as a weakening of an already-troubled school system. The battle lines were drawn in legislatures and the mass media, especially after Minnesota in 1991 passed legislation to create charter schools.

What was unfortunate was that the opponents did not realize and anticipate that the funding argument was, so to speak, an Achilles' heel because those in favor of charter schools could and did proclaim that despite not inconsiderable increased funding for school improvement, little improvement had been demonstrated. Was that not reason enough, they claimed, to justify supporting an innovation which held out the promise of demonstrating that if successful it would stimulate school systems to change in significant ways? After all, the proponents argued, a charter school would be approved—free from the bureaucratic constraints under which existing schools operated—only if it had a truly distinctive *educational* rationale that would make for better *educational* outcomes. I italicize educational to emphasize that the bottom line by which they would ultimately be judged would be essentially educational in nature. If charter schools would have no "educational lessons" to offer school systems, it would be another chapter in the book of well-intentioned but flawed reform efforts. The oppositional stance of the teacher unions (and more than a few parents) to charter school legislation was perceived by many people as symptomatic of the resistance of educators to reformation of the status quo.

What questions could have, should have, the opponents of charter schools asked about how to influence charter school legislation? That is a question about political strategy and it is one which the educational community had learned the hard way. The myth that the political and educational systems could be kept apart was long embraced by educators until the early years after World War II when myth clashed with social-political realities and myth was exposed for what it was: myth. Choosing a political strategy requires choice among alternative possibilities. It is never the case that there is one and only one course of action. And what is decisive in making a choice is how you answer this question: What are the degree and sources of strength of those you oppose? In the case of charter schools the initiative was coming from state governors and legislatures responding to fiscal and public pressures for action to do something to improve educational outcomes, to stop the spiral of increasing the educational budget with no apparent positive consequences. That goal reflected an assumption or conclusion that few public officials said out loud: The existing educational system was allergic to innovations to improve it. If you wish to innovate, you had best demonstrate it outside of the existing system; the existing system was unrescuable. *The concept of charter schools was the most radical challenge ever to the existing system.* More than that, the initiatives of state governors and legislatures reflected the dissatisfactions of a large segment of the citizenry with the inadequacies of past reform efforts. In short, the political support for charter school legislation was the opposite of piddling. The opponents of the legislation initially adapted a strategy of total opposition followed by one the intent of which was to introduce clear constraints on the fiscal resources any charter school would be given (about which I will say more in later pages).

Was there another strategy that was more *proactive* than reactive, more *conservative* and *socially responsible*, more likely to provide a *sound basis* for the application of a possible good idea to the arena of schools generally? Put in another way, can we test the value of the concept of charter schools in a way to give us grounds either to accept or reject them as a means of reforming education? The advocates for charter schools were proceeding on hope; they could provide no empirical basis for that hope. There is little or nothing wrong with hope as long as you realize that hope has at some point to be tested in the real world before you seek to spread it widely as a matter of policy. That was a point the opponents of charter schools never seriously considered if only because they responded (understandably) to the implicit and explicit criticisms of schools the legislation represented. The irony is that, generally speaking, school personnel were themselves critical of how schools were organized and administered and why changing them cosmetically was an exercise in futility, a confirmation of the maxim that no good deed goes unpunished. Far more than a few school personnel had given up hope that schools would on their own change in any non-cosmetic way. What I am saying here is that opponents and proponents were not far apart in their judgment about the capacity of schools to reform themselves.

Let me propose an alternative strategy the opponents of charter schools could have adopted, a strategy that would have made clear one of the most egregious flaws in the proposed legislation. The strategy would have involved the following:

1. Stating clear and loud that past efforts to improve educational outcomes had met with little success. The reasons are several and complicated but certainly one of them was *not* that school personnel were perversely opposed to change.

2. The concept of charter schools had the virtue of identifying one of the major obstacles to change: The traditions and culture of schools contained major barriers to innovations, especially innovations which involved altering power relationships and decision-making processes. For example, although teachers are by far the largest group in schools, their ideas, attitudes, and experience play little or no role in formulating proposals for reform. Teachers are asked or mandated to implement reforms for which they had no input. And that is

no less true for parents and others in the community who have a vested interest in school improvement.

3. It should go without saying that charter schools should be selected and supported if (a) they have a distinctive organizational and educational rationale that gives promise of improving outcomes and (b) they are given the freedom to demonstrate they can accomplish their goals.

4. Because one of the stated purposes of charter schools is that if successful they will have a positive influential impact on existing schools, it is essential that ways be developed whereby *informal* relationships between personnel in charter schools and those in "regular" schools can be ongoing, without impinging on the freedom of charter schools to do what they said they would do. Without such informal relationships charter schools become places isolated from the educational system they hope to influence. It sets the stage for a repetition of what has plagued past reform efforts: importing a reform which is strange, or unfamiliar, or not understood and, therefore, arouses anxiety and resistance. In addition, it is justified to assume that creating, implementing, and sustaining a charter school will be a complicated affair if only because charter school teachers, principals, and governing boards have had no previous experience in creating such schools. It is crucial that what they do and learn be known in some form and to some minimal degree to voluntary representatives from regular schools. Without such informal forums the hoped-for impact of charter schools on the existing system will be minimal or nonexistent.

5. Precisely because the concept of charter schools is new and untried, they should be required and given the funds to keep a detailed chronicle of their activities, problems, decisions, and changes in organization and rationale. Without such a chronicle we will never have a basis for judging why one charter school achieved its goals to the extent that it did and why

another charter school failed or fell far short of its mark. Such a chronicle is crucial if we seek, as we should, to use experience to alter, refine, and improve charter schools that may be created in the future; and, no less important, it should become part of the policy discussion about whether the charter school legislation should be scrapped or significantly changed. At the present time we *hope* charter schools will be productive of new knowledge and practice. That hope places on us the obligation to have a built-in chronicling and evaluation of the dynamics of the first generation of charter schools. The chronicling and evaluating should be done "for the record" and *not* as an intrusive means of influencing what the charter school personnel have decided or will decide to do. They retain the freedom to implement their organizational and educational rationale as they see fit.

6. Because we are embarking on a new venture we should begin with a small number of schools, perhaps a handful, which although few in number will allow us to get our bearings. We should regard these schools as pilot studies from which we can learn whether we can or should increase the number of charter schools. These pilot schools are model A, just as the Wright brothers' first plane that stayed aloft (even briefly) was a model A, that demonstrated what no one had thought possible and that led to improved models B, C, D, and so on.

7. The funding of charter schools should in no way be at the expense of existing school systems. That is to say, the per capita amount the state allots for each student in its public schools will follow each child whose parents will enroll him or her in a charter school. That reduces the budget of the existing school system, which regards its present funding as inadequate. Therefore, the state should reimburse the system so that it cannot claim that the charter schools are being supported at the expense of existing schools, a claim which if not respected will *predictably* create an adversarial gulf between

the two with the adverse consequence that existing school systems will be unreceptive to whatever the outcomes of charter schools are; and we should not be surprised if they seek to undermine them. This possibility itself undermines the hope that charter schools will have a positive impact on existing schools. Any other funding policy is self-defeating.

What the reader has to ask is this question: Is the strategy I have sketched unreasonable? And by unreasonable I mean that it fails to respect and take into account the vested interests of both opponents and proponents of charter school legislation. And I also mean by unreasonable that it fails to protect the public from untested proposals that may be disappointing in their outcomes, costly, a source of divisiveness, and contribute to the strength of those who regard our schools as lost causes. Obviously, I do not regard my sketchy proposal as unreasonable. What is equally obvious is that the sketchy proposal reflects the spirit and rationale of the way that *any* reform should be scrutinized, tested, and judged. And let us not ignore the law of unintended consequences: No reform, like a new drug or medical procedure, may be devoid of side effects and therefore, we are obliged to identify those side effects, determine whether they are outweighed by benefits, or decide that the cost-benefit analysis indicates that, however well-intentioned, the reform does not warrant continued support.

We did not get to the moon because the country and its political leaders thought it was a good idea. We got to the moon because decades of research had demonstrated that enough knowledge had been obtained to justify the attempt to place man on the moon without sacrifice of life. And that justification was based on a long history of diverse studies which failed and gave rise to further studies to avoid the sources of failure and inadequate knowledge. So, when President Kennedy in his inaugural address said that by the end of the decade we would place a man on the moon, he was not being rhetorical or resorting to expression of unrealistic hope. There was tested evidence that the venture was *practical.* It should not go unnoticed that there were opponents to the venture who felt that the size of NASA's budget negatively affected dealing with more immediate "earthly" problems like poverty, racism, etc. You could say that we got to the moon because we had sufficient knowledge to get there, and that kind and quality of knowledge were not in evidence for our earthly problems. The educational arena is a good example. The post-World War II era can rightly be called the era of educational reform. If you were to chronicle the many and diverse educational reforms proposed and/or implemented in that era, it would require several thick volumes. And, yet, the number of reforms which have passed muster probably are less than the fingers on one hand; the others have passed into the history of well-intentioned failures from which we have learned far less than we should have learned. Charter schools are the current, much-heralded educational reform, having opponents and proponents, each group defending its position passionately. As I said earlier, they have one thing in common: Each acknowledges that educational reform should be a top priority on the national agenda. And, as I have also pointed out, both groups are well aware that the charter school movement, initiated largely by state governors and legislatures, has garnered the support of many parents and other advocacy groups. Proponents can present no evidence to justify the claim that charter schools will accomplish intended goals. Opponents can present no evidence that charter schools will not accomplish those goals to any significant degree. Both groups, of course, will disagree with what I have just said. To put it baldly and succinctly, both groups substitute opinion for facts or credible evidence. Question: Should not one do pilot studies in a way that would provide a basis for judging whether the concept of charter schools has the potential to achieve its purposes? Is it asking too much to expect that we can get agreement about what constitutes credible evidence of accomplishments? Are we to be content only with opinion in matters of school change?

Let us now turn to the features of the first cohort of charter schools, a cohort consisting of approximately two to three thousand schools funded largely by states, with additional funding from the federal government and foundations. As we shall see in the following chapters, these features do not reflect the spirit and substance of my sketch of an alternative approach.

CHAPTER 5

CHARTER SCHOOLS:
INITIAL OBSERVATIONS

In all states with charter schools the state department of education invited applications, making clear that approval required, at a minimum, that its founders must consist of (a) largely credentialed educators, parents, and members of the larger community promoting (b) a distinctive, well-described educational program and goals and articulating (c) by what criteria or means they will demonstrate the degree of their accomplishments. In some states—like Arizona, Connecticut, and New York—a charter could be given by more than one state agency, a practice that clearly indicated that criteria or approval and future judgments of accomplishments would vary and make comparability of results problematic. In addition, far more often than not the interval between approval and starting date could be as little as a few months. That small interval has to be understood in light of the pressure on state agencies "to get started," to implement the legislation spearheaded by governors and legislative leaders. It is an unwritten rule in public bureaucracies that if legislation has provided funds for a program, you commit these funds as quickly as possible.

In one state I was asked to advise an agency about what the predictable problems would be in creating charter schools. So I advised. At the end of my visit in late February I was astonished to be told that the choice of schools had been pretty much determined and that they would be opened at the beginning of the new school year in early September. Every suggestion I had made to them clearly indicated that such a time perspective was wildly unrealistic. But they were under the gun to act and act they did with untoward results. My suggestions were not dreamed up but based on what I had learned from charter school personnel in other states. I learned a lot but for the sake of brevity I will paraphrase what they said: "When we wrote our application we wrote what we thought the state department wanted to hear. What we wrote were generalizations in which we believed, but it was not a detailed or specific plan of action. We were far from certain that our application would be approved; we were right in assuming that there was not enough funding to support other than a low percentage of approvable applications. So, if we wrote our application and were approved, we would then deal with the nitty-gritty details: selecting teachers, students, principal; where we would find adequate, affordable, housing for the school; the extent and ways we would use computers for learning; the way in which the relationship between the mandated advisory-governing board and school personnel would be structured; the different ways we would test the progress of students; the substance of our disciplinary code; and how we would relate to and exploit community resources. We did not have the time to work out and get agreement on these and other details. Remember that the founding group consisted largely of working people who at best could get together two, maybe three, evenings a week for at most a couple of hours. We had a deadline to meet and what essentially happened by necessity was that the informal leader of the group was asked to write the application. Also keep in mind that not all members of the founding group had known or worked with one another and when they did begin to meet it was clear that different members had different ideas and agendas for the charter school. We were both gratified and surprised when our application was approved, but when it was, reality hit us. Starting a school from scratch is monumentally complicated, especially when there is time pressure. One of the first problems that hit us was the gulf between the funds we were given and what we wanted to do. We could not put the school anywhere. We had to meet safety regulations, be in decent repair, and be ample enough to meet the needs of future students in grades that would have to be added to make it the school we said we would develop. If, for example, we started with students in grades one and two, we would in subsequent years have them in grades three and four as well as new grade one and grade two cohorts. Where do you find such a space? Given the funding we could count on, we could not be choosy. Money was a problem from day one. So was time, and when opening day arrived we were tired, nervous wrecks."

If the founder of a charter school had no personal experience creating a new setting, that was also the case for those who were responsible for approving them. Here one could ask this question: In light of the fact that in the post-World War II era thousands of new "traditional" schools had been built, what had been learned that was applicable to charter schools? Granted that on the surface new and traditional schools are not comparable to charter schools. That does not necessarily mean that nothing can be learned from the former usable by the latter. Having lived through and closely observed the creation of new traditional schools, the answer to the question is clearly in the affirmative. In all the traditional schools I observed there were several features, fateful ones, that have never been acknowledged in published form and, therefore, could not alert both policy makers and charter school advocates to the practical consequences of these features. Here are several features:

1. When a new traditional school was to be built and opened, it was not conveyed to the public that it would be a clone of existing schools. By virtue of the new and presumably innovative facilities the school would in some ways make for a superior educational experience for students. The choice of principal for the new school was, in part at least, intended to insure that he or she was someone who would capitalize on the opportunity to improve or enrich the educational experience. From the standpoint of the appointed principal, the

new school was a plum, a golden, much-fantasized opportunity to create something new and better than his previous experience in schools had been. Just as parents seek to avoid with their second child the mistakes they made with their first one, the principal of the new school wanted to avoid what he saw as the demerits of the schools in which he had taught; within existing constraints the new school would be a "better" school. Just as the founders of a charter school are going to do what they said would be different from and superior in educational outcomes of existing schools, the new principal of the new traditional sought to do the same, albeit what he wanted to demonstrate was less radical and not in any clear way a challenge to the existing system.

2. Of the six new traditional schools I closely observed, the choice of principal was never made before midwinter of the school year preceding the year the school was to be opened and running. In all but one instance the principal had either been a teacher in the system or a principal. In one case the principal had that role in another school system. I need not go into the myriad of details a principal of a new school confronts; they vary from the piddling to the crucial and they are very time-consuming. For all practical purposes the appointed principal had two jobs. Not until the summer before the school would open would the individual totally become immersed in what needed to be done. None of the principals of these new traditional schools looks back at the interval between appointment and school opening with anything resembling fond memories but rather as a period of anxiety, problems, and frustration. As I noted earlier, in the case of charter schools, the interval between the approval of the application and the opening of the school is rarely more than six months, but unlike instances of the new traditional schools, it is incomparably more trying, if only because they do not have the constraints—the rules and regulations, traditions, and resources—an existing system imposes and which school personnel comfortably take for granted and that clearly convey

messages about what you can do and what is off-limits. The founders of a charter school are in the same situation as the founding fathers at the constitutional convention in 1787: How do we forge a document that will insure the achievement of our values and goals? What will our charter be and why? What resources do we have and what additional ones will we require? And they knew full well that they were creating something unique in human history. They had overthrown an existing, foreign-imposed form of government. They were starting, so to speak, from scratch.

3. The principals of these new traditional schools considered that their most important task was the selection of a teaching staff, priority to be given to teachers then in the system. The single, most important criterion the principals employed was whether a teacher would fit in with the distinctive features the principal wanted to have. Some of the teachers the principal selected were known to her although the teachers often did not know each other. And more often than not the principal had not been in the same school with the teachers she knew and selected. In all of the schools the teachers selected were not given formal notification of selection until a month or two before the end of the school year. The principals requested funding to make planning possible and a "get to know each other" process in the summer for at least a month before the school would open. That request was denied. At the most the teachers met for a week or so before school opened. Let me just say that by the end of the second week of school two things were apparent. The first was that they had not anticipated certain predictable problems of a logistical or scheduling nature, discipline, a variety of questions from parents, teacher illness, etc. Second, and important for the future, it became apparent that teachers varied considerably in personality, interpersonal style, educational philosophy, and flexibility, and that not all teachers liked each other; it was also apparent that some principals reacted to the pressures of opening the school in autocratic and insensitive ways, at least

in the eyes of some teachers. At the end of the school year, whatever the intended innovative features of the school, they were hard to discern; they were traditional—traditional schools. What I have just described was far more glaring and apparent in many charter schools. They did not have a school; they had to create it in short order. The realities of the task brought out differences of opinions about allocation of limited resources, governance, parental role, leadership and decision making, curriculum, and more, much more. A complicating factor was that because charter schools were not regarded favorably by the existing school system and many teachers were unwilling to move in that new direction, a significant number of teachers available to be selected were young, inexperienced, but motivated. They came from near and far, and in more than a few cases had met with the founder for less than a day. That these teachers did not really know what was expected of them, why days would be so long and arduous, why funds could not be available for certain instructional materials and technology, why available space would be inadequate, why there would be differences of opinion, among teachers and between teachers and the governing board—these and more were not anticipated by the teachers, and neither were they anticipated by the founders. I have met with charter school personnel and their governing boards and no one has ever denied that developing and opening a charter school was one of the destabilizing experiences of their lives. No charter school recovered fully from that early period, some (I would say more) never recovered, and an undetermined number were terminated.

What I am suggesting is that there potentially was a body of past experience with opening traditional schools that could have been of practical use in formulating charter school legislation. But that experience never got written up; it remains as memories in the minds of those who had the experience. That has long been a characteristic of efforts at educational reform. We do not get the details and in judging reform the reader should never forget to ask for the details, which is where the devils reside (I will have more to say about this in the next chapter).

The points of all this are several. The first, and one that should have been obvious to policy makers, is that conceiving, developing, and opening a charter school is a very, very personally, interpersonally, and conceptually demanding task. It is not, so to speak, a piece of cake, a routine engineering process. And it is difficult even when conditions are more favorable than has been the case for the average charter school. Precisely because it is so difficult, and because charter schools are a source of controversy, chronicling their developmental history is a necessity, not a luxury. When we have to pass judgment on charter schools, that history is crucial if we are to learn what we need to learn about improving them or terminating them. *The sad fact is that no state has appropriated funds to make possible such chronicles.* It is worse than sad, it is *inexcusable.* As matters stand now we will have no secure basis for rendering judgment. We will be unable to identify what contributed to acceptable or unacceptable outcomes.

Another point concerns funding. Each charter school gets the same per capita payment that a traditional school is given, although some states have increased it a bit for charter schools. Why the same? The argument was that charter schools should demonstrate that they do a superior job with the same amount of money traditional schools are given. That is a strange argument because unlike charter schools, who have to locate space (and usually have to renovate it) and pay rent, when a traditional school is built it is the state that pays a good deal of the costs. But there is a more basic issue. The potential virtue of charter schools is that they are intended to demonstrate educational strategies and innovations that are more effective than those employed in traditional schools with similar children. The important question is not whether that can be demonstrated on the cheap, so to speak, but rather whether we may learn things that can be applied to and be more cost-effective than what is done in traditional schools. And, as I have emphasized, no opponent or proponent of charter schools has denied that traditional schools are, generally speaking, not cost-effective enterprises and in the case of urban schools they are dramatically the opposite of cost-effective. And still another argument against the funding policy for charter schools is that they are so new and untried that one has to expect they will encounter unanticipated problems for which the usual per capita allotment may be insufficient and will affect outcomes which may otherwise have been achieved. This is in no way to suggest that charter schools be given a blank check. I am asserting that the present funding policy sets the future stage on which proponents can claim that the funding policy contributed to failures. May I point out that current advocacy for smaller class size has, where implemented, cost a great deal of money, justified by what people regard as self-evidently the case that educational outcomes will be significantly improved. I have argued in my previous writings that what seems self-evidently true to most people is not so to me and, therefore, I predict the outcomes will not be as dramatic as people expect. But in the case of the charter schools from which we may learn some important things about school learning, a somewhat more liberal funding policy was rejected. From whatever I have learned about existing charter schools, it is clear that funding has been a major handicap to doing what they want to do. And one can assume that the failure of the policy makers to require a chronicling-developmental process was because to do it well would have been costly. Need I expand on the saying that it is another example of being penny-wise and pound foolish, a saying long applicable to the support of educational reform. When charter schools came up on the educational horizon, it was my hope that the number of charter schools would be very small, perhaps no more than a handful in each state, but that they be well funded and very carefully chronicled. That, of course, is not what happened. Arizona is an egregious example because in the first two years after the legislation it approved upward of two hundred charter schools. At the present time the average number of charter schools in a state is somewhere between fifteen and twenty (and climbing). I must repeat: Funding has been one of the major problems of charter schools. I would say that it is the most important problem because of its effect on two other major problems of charter schools.

What literature is currently available on charter schools justifies the conclusion that issues of governance have been a problem. (That this was predictable I discuss in the next chapter.) Governing boards consist of people of diverse backgrounds and life experiences. In almost all cases a small majority on the board are educators. As I said earlier, no one had experience starting a new school for which he was responsible. When, as it did, it became quickly evident that there would be a disparity between their funds and what they had hoped to do, they confronted a number of difficult decisions, e.g., should they choose this site or that one which was less costly but less adequate; should they increase the number of students they had planned for; could they afford to seek to attract experienced teachers in light of a limited budget; should they cut back on the number of computers they hoped to purchase; in the event that the number of parents enrolling their children was less than what had been planned for, would that affect the budget, and how should they handle that; if the number of applicants was greater than planned, what criteria for selection would be used to avoid the criticism that they chose the "best and the brightest," the least likely to cause problems? Should they use a lottery system which critics would say is fair but would mean that the school may get a variety of students some of whom may have problems requiring special knowledge and personnel; what kinds of educational decisions should the principal and teachers be free to make without discussing them with the board, which can have complications for the budget; and by whom and how will fiscal responsibility be insured? There are more questions but I have given enough to make the obvious point that major educational decisions have budgetary consequences, especially when the budget is limited and there are no backups. It is these kinds of decisions that brought to the fore the fact that there was far from agreement among governing board members about how to deal with these issues. This, in more than a few cases, produced divisiveness, questions about leadership, rivalries. I have to assume that in an undetermined number of charter schools these issues had no destabilizing consequences, but in the few observations that have been published, the governance issue is perceived as a source of major concern. Here are some excerpts from a study of five charter schools in Massachusetts by Abbey Weiss of the Institute for Responsive Education at Northeastern University (1997):

> *Governance.* In several of the schools we visited, governance was highlighted by the school leaders and staff alike as the major barrier to effective implementation of their educational plans.
>
> At charter schools, every policy, every position, everything the school does for the first time must be created. So decisions, both small and large, need to be made frequently and should be made efficiently. Without a well-defined structure in place for decision-making, the first few months, indeed, the first year, can be extremely difficult.
>
> The most significant barrier within governance concerns role definitions and decision-making. Many school leaders and teachers are unsure of their job descriptions (one principal had just received his job description after 19 months on the job) and the parameters of their jobs. Which responsibilities are theirs, and which belong to the board? Who should be setting policies? Which policies are to be classroom policies, and which are to be school-wide? How can collaborative decision-making be implemented efficiently?
>
> Students discussed the difficulties encountered with respect to the governance structure. At one school, where students are very involved in decision-making, one student told us, "I wish they wouldn't make decisions and then ask our opinion of them; I wish they would give us a chance to help make the decisions in the first place." This comment suggests that students are very involved in the governance of the school and felt ownership over the

process. At this same school, observation of a governance group which included students and staff showed that student participation and input is taken seriously. But at this school, governance and decision-making is tricky.

Teachers commented that they feel conflicted about the level of student involvement because it often interferes with their ability to discipline. They respect the students and do not want to undermine their participation in the governance of the school, however they need to make clear to them that the teachers are still the authorities. One teacher said, "I'm not sure what my roles here are. Are students and teachers equal? What rules are negotiable?"

At another school, one parent, who is also a board member, commented, "Our governance is an untried model. We had no policies in place and no job descriptions. We need to decide who should do what. These roles need to be defined, so that we can start writing policies."

School climate and culture. Another organizational issue, related to governance, found at several of these charter schools is creating a school climate and culture that is based on respect and trust but which also sets appropriate limits for students. These schools are facing a difficult dilemma: they want to create a discipline policy that establishes a stable school environment but that is not so restrictive that it conflicts with the philosophy of the school. Schools are finding this balance difficult to achieve. Especially in those schools in which students are actively involved in governance, teachers are having difficulty drawing the parameters of the roles of the students.

As was already mentioned under governance, the climate and culture issue has two sides. One teacher said, "The culture here is both what works best and worst. Because of the free culture, kids have ownership, and that's great. But they show up late and there are no clear consequences. Even though it is prohibited in our constitution, kids can opt out of doing work."

At a couple of schools, we found a lack of a clear vision. At one school, a teacher commented, "We're still figuring out what we're about. We're trying to be about everything all the time, and we are stretched too thin. We lack a clear vision." At another school, when asked, parents could not tell us what the vision of the school was. Parents said, "We're not there yet," and "We have many visions." We found that without a clear vision, schools have a more difficult time with the decision-making processes and policy-setting. A clear vision allows schools to establish predictable policies, as well as expectations for their community members, all of which flow from this common understanding of what the school is about.

Time. All of the teaching staff and principals that we have met with reported that their work hours are long and intense. Despite the fact that these schools are committed to structuring a great deal of common planning/professional development time into the school day, teachers and school leaders spend a considerable amount of time beyond the school day planning and working together on organizational issues. One teacher told us that his board deliberately hired young teachers because teachers in their early twenties are unlikely to have the familial obligations that would keep them from making the enormous time commitment necessary to their charter school positions. Staff burn-out is a major concern.

Time is also an issue during the charter planning process. The time it takes to plan a school is significant, and most states do not account for this in their charter application schedule. Several founders told us that they found it difficult to plan the school carefully during the application process, and, as a result, they wrote very broad applications in an effort to please the reviewers. When their applications were accepted, they were forced to try to implement their very ambitious plans. School planners do have (in some states) the option of delaying opening their school for a year after their application is accepted, however, there are limited state funds to support that year of planning.

Isolation. These educators are creating new schools and are undertaking this monumental task by themselves (by definition, they do not receive district support).

Charter schools often feel isolated from their communities, and many are not assessing the valuable resources in the community of charter schools. Charter schools could benefit from this interaction in order to address their many common issues while also recognizing and maintaining their core individuality. When we asked principals about their networking with other charter school personnel, they acknowledged that charter schools are not networking in a meaningful way. A few of the school heads meet informally, but for the most part, school leaders report that they are not in conversation with other schools. And a couple of principals did not express much interest in this prospect either. The schools do send a staff person to the occasional conferences or meetings, but these are not regular, and, for the most part, there does not appear to be much opportunity for sharing (pp. 15–16).

Money becomes a factor in those charter schools which start with students of more than two or three grades. If there is anything common to application for charter status, it is the explicit emphasis on the individual attention that will be given students. It is that emphasis that is influential for many parents' decision to enroll their children. Given the fact that budgets are tight and the expectation that some students will present one or another type of learning difficulty, plus the turmoil of opening a new school, the size of the initial cohorts can contain unplanned-for problems. That is especially the case in the larger charter schools where they were confronted with students whose grade placement was wrong and/or who needed a special education program. In other words, these students—and you do not need many of them—needed specialized programs and services the school did not have or they required teaching time an already-overburdened teaching staff hardly had. And in some instances the student required the expertise of special personnel the school could not afford.

Some parents complained, of course. The governing board could do little to provide the special services, and the teachers were, as the teachers often are, asked to do more with less.

Nothing I have said in this chapter was intended to "prove" that these new schools would not meet their goals after three to five years. You could argue that once the shakedown experience was over they progressed as they had hoped. But you could also argue that the shakedown had lasting negative effects. In that event, how would we know which of the different sources of a negative factor (or factors) provides us the kind of information from which we can learn usable, practical knowledge for future policy decisions? If we have no detailed developmental chronicle, we are left with opinion, a very frail basis for policy decisions.

Now let us pose the issue in a somewhat narrower way by asking this question: In terms of achievement test scores, on what basis will we be able to decide to what degree a charter school achieved its purposes? At the very least no charter school would claim success if its students did not year by year show "normal" development on achievement tests. Reading charter school applications, however, you almost always find the prediction that the *rate* of academic progress for a significant number of students will increase over the years. It would be unusual in the extreme if all (or almost all) would show such an increase, but on average a significant number of students would be expected to show clear increases. Are we to be satisfied with such findings and conclude that the school was a success? The only conclusion to which one can legitimately come is that the school *did not fail*; it does not speak to the claim that the students did *better* than they would have if they had remained in their regular school, a claim made implicitly or explicitly by advocates of charter schools. And let us not forget that whatever success of an academic and organizational nature charter schools would or could demonstrate, that success would or should have an *impact* on *conventional schools*.

How might this be tested? That is not an easy task but I shall suggest one approach which will give the reader a sense of what might be tried; more correctly, what should have been funded and tried.

The core idea of my suggestion is the question: What would constitute a contrast or comparison group to contrast with the experimental group which is, of course, charter school students? One way is that for every charter school student we select a student from the *same classroom* in the *same school* which the charter school student had attended, matching on the basis of *achievement and intelligence test scores, socioeconomic background, age,* and *gender.* Practically speaking, that may or will not be an easy task; matching students never is easy. The point is that you try to make as good matches as available data permits. A less than perfect match is better than having no match at all when the claim is made that one expects charter schools to demonstrate superior results. When the predictably less than perfect matches are made, you collect year by year data relevant to the purposes of the match, and you do that for as long as the charter indicated it would take for it to be fairly judged. Most charter schools are approved for at least three to five years before they come up for formal review: to continue or be terminated. Without matching data that decision will be made on the basis of personal opinion rather than on objective or semiobjective data, given the fact that many charter schools have had a troubled existence in their first year or so; it has been my opinion that a three-year initial period is much less fair than a five-year period during which the start-up problems of the first year or so may have been overcome. There are administrators and teachers in *conventional* schools who have participated in a reform effort under pressure to show quick results, pressures that were unrealistic in terms of the complexity of the reform effort. What too many policy makers have difficulty understanding is that it is relatively easy to proclaim or mandate a new policy but to personnel "in the trenches," implementation of the policy is the opposite of easy.

The advocates of charter schools can with justice criticize my suggestion by saying, "Charter schools were not intended

50

to be like regular schools but to be free to innovate in how and what students learn and to devise ways of evaluating the degree to which they learned what we hoped they would learn. What we are trying to do should not and cannot be measured by conventional tests. Critical thinking, independent thinking, doing experiments and special projects, presenting and defending the results of projects of special interest to them, amassing a portfolio of their work which others will critique— these are activities conventional tests tell us little about; they simply are not relevant to what our students will be thinking about and doing. Cognitive abilities and their nurturing are what we are interested in. Therefore, the kind of matching you suggest is like comparing apples and oranges. Our students will learn subject matter but not for the purpose of regurgitating it on a conventional test. We will develop means for judging what they do. We are not opposed to subject matter but subject matter is not the be-all or end-all of schooling."

I am sure that any teacher who reads the above criticism will agree that conventional tests are unrevealing about many things the teacher has observed and considers important. And in these days of raised standards and accountability (with potential negative consequences for how teachers will be judged) teachers resent the worship of tests and "teaching to the test." Those readers who are opposed to charter schools should reflect on the fact that the pressure to conform to narrow criteria for judging student learning is one factor which has galvanized the charter school movement.

However, the criticism of my suggestion requires that we ask this question: How reliable and valid are the judgments of portfolios and independent projects of student learning? Would external judges use similar criteria for judging the quality of those activities? Would their judgments agree with those of charter school personnel? It is not being a carping critic to say that charter school personnel may not be as objective as they should be because they have such a personal stake in demonstrating the quality of their program. If conventional tests have their drawbacks, should we not expect the criteria

51

for judgments that charter schools employ will have drawbacks requiring that they be identified and improved?

Developing new ways to judge new activities is no easy task. It will take time and money, which no charter school has. It would require, in addition, a kind of technical sophistication they also lack. I am not directing blame at or derogating school personnel but rather the policy makers and charter school lobbyists for being blind to these issues and passing legislation which does a disservice to a much-heralded educational reform intended to demonstrate with credible evidence that it has been successful in this or that way to this or that degree. Good intentions and fervent hope are, like love, no guarantee whatsoever that purposes will be achieved.

What I have said in these pages is applicable to any educational reform, not only to charter schools. Educational reform is a serious affair intended to impact positively on the lives of students, parents, school personnel, and conventional schools. Reform is too important to be implemented without procedures that give us knowledge we can use for future policy decisions. Reform efforts in the post-World War II era have been, to indulge understatement, many in number. There has been pathetically little that has stood the test of time and results. By any cost-benefit analysis these reforms have not only not passed muster but we have failed to ask those questions the answers to which might have contributed to better results.

I have already said that in principle I have been a proponent of charter schools although I have been forced to conclude and predict that they will fall far short of their mark. I hope I am wrong, but I doubt that I am. In the next chapter I will use my personal history in order to indicate that long before charter schools came on the educational scene there was a body of experience that could have put charter schools in a more illuminating and less divisive context and let them stand more of a chance to influence schools as we know them. As I shall endeavor to demonstrate, charter schools contain predictable problems and processes one finds in many arenas of social living. It has taken a long time for the educational community to understand that schools are not unique organizations, they are just different. To claim they are unique organizations is to miss a truly basic point of how similar they are to other forms of organization.

CHAPTER 6

CHARTER SCHOOLS, MARRIAGES, AND MERGERS

From the very start of the charter school movement, judgments were starkly polarized to a degree that could lead one to conclude that the fate of our educational system was at stake. Opponents saw charter schools as unjustified criticism and an assault on existing schools. Proponents argued that the existing system needed to be reformed and that charter schools would demonstrate the direction that reform would take. Opponents asserted that the existing system was capable of reforming itself if given more freedom and funding to initiate change. Proponents could and did argue, "We have heard all that before. Funding did mightily increase but there is little or nothing to show for it." Opponents never dealt directly with that retort. The historical record was not on their side. What they had to offer by way of reform was vague and unconvincing to political leaders under pressure to take bold steps for reform. It was as if the opponents knew what they were against but not what they were for. Proponents knew what they were for and why but mammothly glossed over and underestimated the difficulty of creating, implementing, and sustaining a type of new school with which they had had no experience. The concept of a charter school was relatively clear but when you go from concept to action and the realities of organizational living and human relationships, you confront a host of problems that should have been predicted but were not, and that is the major mistake charter school advocates made. They had an egregiously oversimple understanding of what creating a charter school entailed. They made it sound as if creating a charter school was like building a bridge, largely an engineering problem.

I said that charter school advocates had nothing to say about the predictable problems charter schools would confront. If these problems are predictable, why were they ignored? The short answer is that charter schools were seen as a unique form of human organization and experience bearing no relationship to personal experience in noneducational spheres of living. By using the label "charter school" it was intended to distinguish such a school from regular schools. That intention was as accurate as it was understandable. But labels have the unintended consequence of closing our minds to the possibility that other phenomena in our personal experience to which we have given a different label may have been relevant to that new label. Labels are a mixed blessing; they are meant to differentiate among phenomena but they run the danger of overlooking similarities. Let me give a longer and more concrete answer to what I consider to be a truly crucial point that both opponents and proponents failed to recognize. The point, once made, is a glimpse of the obvious.

Question: Of what larger category of human experience are charter schools instances? That category is what I have termed as *the creation of settings* (Sarason 1972). And by creation of settings I mean *when two or more people get together in new and sustained relationships to achieve agreed-upon goals.* For example, when legislation was initially passed for Head Start, it meant that several thousand new settings were to be created. Each program would have a governing board, set policies, choose a site, select staff, and develop a stimulating educational (broadly speaking) program that would prevent student problems and failure when these preschoolers entered their public schools. The interval between legislative enactment and action to create these settings varied from several weeks to a few months, and that fact is testimony enough to expect trouble ahead. There were power struggles among community groups about representation and leadership of the program;

whether it should be related to, overseen by, or located in an existing school; and criteria for selection of students and staff. It was almost immediately apparent that funding was inadequate for achievement of purposes at the same time that there was little clarity about the relationship between purposes and the forging of a concrete program. And it was almost immediately apparent that funding would be a problem. Having at the time personally observed several of these programs, and talked with others who observed other programs, I feel justified in saying that many of these programs were organizational and interpersonal messes. No one claims that Head Start has been a rousing success and what data are available are less than convincing, if only because the purposes of many programs became more modest. This does not mean that Head Start children derived no benefits from their preschool experience, but it does mean that in terms of preventing school problems and failures—the major justification for the program—Head Start is disappointing. The reasons are many and more complex than I have indicated. I have used Head Start as an example of creating settings which from their birth were plagued by problems, many of which were predictable to anyone knowledgeable about the inner-city areas of our cities. Good intentions are not enough. Between good intentions and action is a road full of potholes about such matters as governance, power, authority, money, leadership, interpersonal style, and time perspective.

Marriage (formal or informal) is the smallest instance of creating a new setting. One might think that creating a setting consisting of two people who presumably know and love each other would run a course radically different from that of charter schools and Head Start. Divorce statistics obviously suggest otherwise. You could fill a good-sized building with the articles and books on marriage and divorce. And if you included novels, plays, and movies, you would have to enlarge the building. Here I wish only to list the most frequent themes in that vast literature that are similar to what has been described about charter schools.

1. What you come to know and feel about a person before marriage overlaps with but is not identical with what you come to know and feel after marriage. Intimacies before marriage take place in contexts that are not the same—or they do not feel the same—as the context of marriage.

2. Before marriage the relationship is based on the assumption that love (like good intentions) is enough to overcome whatever problems will arise. An additional assumption is that the two people are in agreement about values and purposes. They take that agreement for granted. In the abstract they know there will be problems but it is literally inconceivable—at least difficult to imagine—that they will not find ways to overcome the problems. They are aware of the divorce rate and loving each other as they do, they will be able to remain married.

3. It is inevitable—and I use that word advisedly—that as people embark on marriage they begin to see themselves and their relationships in new ways. These new ways may be experienced as positive or negative. In the many marriages which have a short life these new ways are upsetting, disillusioning, and cause for second thoughts about the wisdom of having married their spouse. At least to one of them it seems clear that either (a) he or she really had not known his or her spouse or (b) he or she really had misjudged him- or herself in regard to the confines of marriage, to what he or she thought about the purposes of marriage.

4. Every new setting is related to, impacts on, and in turn is impacted by outside forces: parents, in-laws, extended family, friends, work setting, and the state of the economy. I leave it to the reader to figure out how and why any of these externalities may be benign and supportive or stressful and destabilizing for a marriage. No new setting exists in a social world organized to prevent differences between its members or the exacerbation of minor problems into bigger ones.

5. When contemplating marriage the couple does not think in terms of governance and leadership. In the old days it was taken for granted who would make which decisions. The husband had his turf and responsibilities and the wife had hers; ultimate decisions about money and resources were, on the surface at least, the husband's. That did not mean that the wife graciously went along with the husband's role and decisions. In subtle and not so subtle ways she would seek to influence those decisions but always aware of the rules of marital relationship. It is a very different story today. Women increasingly see themselves as an equal of men in regard to any major decision; they do not take kindly (as they should not) being "out of the loop" of any major decision. Depending on the personalities of the two, governance and decision making can elicit reactions that bring out in the open a disturbing fact that they never anticipated: Each is not the person he or she had previously known, they do see the world and themselves differently, they are confronting what they never bargained for. These reactions may simmer, fester, or explode.

In the nineteenth century and in the sizzling years of the sixties, a number of communes were created precisely in order to create a setting in which its members could lead the good life as they defined it. With one or two exceptions, these communes were interpersonal, social, organizational disasters. What they all held in common was the myth that possessed of exalted or innovative purposes, prepared to give their all to achieve those purposes, there was no obstacle to achieving those purposes that could not be surmounted. That myth, like many myths, contains a kernel of truth, but it is only a kernel; in their case a kernel which will only sprout and grow if the actors play an appropriately nurturing role. When mountain climbers are asked why they want to climb Mount Everest, they reply, "Because it is there." What they are conveying is that Mount Everest is a major challenge, reaching its top a treasured vision, and success requires the highest degree of determination and motivation. But that answer is woefully incomplete and even misleading because of what it leaves out. And what it leaves out are the answers to these questions: What preparation is necessary if the mountain is to be climbed? What equipment do you need and why? What are the problems you will predictably encounter? What do you know from others or from your previous experience that has influenced how you are planning the ascent? Since you cannot climb the mountain by yourself and you will need a small, core group of assistants whom you will lead, what criteria do you use to select that core group? Because of the many dangers on making the ascent, how do you decide what technical-material resources you will need? When you ask these and other questions, you begin to grasp that climbing the mountain requires more than vision, motivation, and even courage.

Creating a charter school is, like climbing the mountain, an awesomely complicated personal, interpersonal, cognitive, and practical affair. And yet, when you listen to the arguments opponents and proponents of charter schools put forth, that complexity is never recognized or discussed. More correctly, it was not discussed until it became apparent that many charter schools were not sailing on smooth seas.

One more example, again one that on the surface would seem to have nothing to do with creating and sustaining charter schools appropriate to their stated purposes. Labels can obscure as much as or more than they signify.

Most readers will have had no experience with charter schools and will regard them as a kind of new species to which their knowledge and experience have no relevance. That is understandable but such readers are selling themselves short. That is unfortunate because most readers, if only because they read newspapers and magazines, know about mergers in the private and nonprofit sectors in society. By definition a merger is an example of the creation of a new setting in order to achieve agreed-upon goals which each alone could not do. It is a form of marriage, the smallest instance of a new setting. A merger, like marriage, requires far more than the pooling of resources if the agreed-upon goals are to be achieved. Mergers and charter schools are on the surface in different worlds but they share very similar developmental dynamics. Up until recent decades schools were regarded as unique institutions. It is one thing to say they are unique, and therefore, incomparable. It is another thing to say they are different, that they share important features with other complicated organizations. Similarly, mergers and charter schools are, from the standpoint of the creation of settings, not in different worlds.

Mergers, as the reader well knows, have been taking place at a somewhat exponential rate in almost all spheres of social-institutional activity, e.g., business, health, publishing, to name a few. However explicit and varied the stated purposes of the merger may be, there is one purpose that is bedrock: The merged organization will be "better" than and "superior" to what the two organizations had heretofore been.

That was the case in the merger of two hospitals very near each other, literally across the street from each other. The merging of the two hospitals would make them more competitive with other health organizations, allow them to survive, and help them to exploit their existing resources more efficiently. There was another feature characteristic of the creation of a new setting. The merger was spearheaded by the leaders of the two hospitals. In my 1972 book I talk of the new setting only in terms of a single leader. What I did not but should have stressed is that in all of the illustrative cases I referred to— including my leadership in creating the Yale Psycho-Educational Clinic—the leader is always dealing with other leaders, so that in my case I had to deal with the chairman, the dean of the graduate school, and the provost at Yale. In a more indirect way I also had to deal with the leaders of community agencies. It was a mistake on my part to convey the impression that the leader of a new setting operates without constraint on some Olympian perch. In the book I emphasize that he or she is constrained by the human dynamics within the setting. I did not (and could not) envision that a time would soon come when the leaders of two settings would agree so frequently to participate in the creation of a new setting.

There is a difference between mergers and absorptions, as in the case of hostile takeovers where there is no intention of creating a new setting. Mergers are instances of creating a new setting which is expected to benefit both parties as in the case of the smallest instance of the creation of a new setting: marriage. I know that asserting entering marriage involves issues and dynamics similar to those in a voluntary corporate merger may strike some people as strange, as equating apples and oranges, but close scrutiny of the marriage-divorce literature (a voluminous one) and the burgeoning one on mergers reveals compelling similarities in substance and process. The expectation of better or superior consequences; the belief that motivation and goodwill are sufficient to overcome obstacles; that verbal agreement on values and purposes means the same thing to the participants; that little or no significant issues surrounding leadership and power will emerge; that personal differences in style, ambition, and future perspective among the participants will be secondary to the overarching concern for the welfare of the setting; that people or forces external to the setting but who are interested in or impacted directly or indirectly by the new setting will not be threats to it; that there are or will be sufficient resources to surmount all difficulties; that whatever problems or conflicts occurred in the "before-the-beginning" phase have been resolved and will not reappear— these are some of the more obvious commonalities between mergers and marriages. You can sum up much of this in this way: The enthusiasm, the fantasy of enduring goodwill and accomplishment of "success," blots out attention to (or mammothly downplays) predictable problems to any venture in which people come together over a sustained period of time to achieve agreed-upon goals. That, it is obvious, is true for marriage, and I predict it will be no less characteristic of mergers.

Back to the merger of two hospitals. For a period of years I was a member of an external advisory committee to one of those hospitals which had a deserved national reputation for the quality of its research, patient care, and the level of job satisfaction of all its employees. Indeed, in a list of the thirty

61

"corporations" reputed to have the highest level of employee satisfaction, this was the only hospital on the list. This did not surprise me because over the years I had met with laundry staff, kitchen help, nurses, ward attendants, lab technicians, physicians, and more. Although the hospital opposed union efforts to organize it, it never went to anything resembling an extreme effort to block or undermine the union's activities. The union has never won an election. I am not alone in the belief that the president-leader of the hospital is in a class by himself in regard to interpersonal sensitivity, direct contact with and direct knowledge of employee feelings, attitudes, and advice (and this is a large hospital in a large city renowned for its hospitals).

When I received the agenda for the most recent meeting, it contained the announcement that we would discuss an agreed-upon merger with a very nearby hospital. Being a devoted reader of the *New York Times* and diverse periodicals, I was aware (how could one not be?) of what has been called "merger mania" and had regretted the fact that I had no opportunity to observe any aspect of the merger process. Some of the accounts I had read were of the gory variety in regard to the turmoil and animosities that preceded and followed the mergers. Needless to say, where a merger has been relatively successful, depending on what you consider to be criteria of success, you are not likely to hear about it if only because it is not considered newsworthy. We know far more about failed than about successful marriages, and that is likely to turn out to be the case in regard to mergers.

In any event, I eagerly looked forward to the meeting. I wrote down several questions to which I hoped I might get at least a partial answer.

1. Who would assume leadership of the merged settings? What was the basis for that choice? Was the decision arrived at without difficulty? Were its implications, near- and long-term, examined in an explicit and forthright manner? How explicit were the altered powers of the new or supplanted

leadership? In the event that problems of power and leadership arise, what mechanisms or forums would exist to deal with them? Or was it that there was no recognition of the possibility that such problems were predictable, or if they did arise, there was the feeling that they could be overcome by goodwill, reason, and selflessness? Was it the case that issues of leadership reflected the strength and role of the two boards of trustees and, to a lesser extent, the two present leaders? In brief, who participated and in what ways in the decision?

2. Immediately below the two top leaders and their boards, each hospital had far from minuscule layers of leaders-managers. What role did they have and when did these people participate in the decision to merge? Among these layers in each hospital, what degree of agreement was obtained about the merger? What questions, problems, predictions, and concerns surfaced and what alternatives, not to the merger itself, but to the details of the agreement, were expressed? Were they presented as a *fait accompli,* and if so, were there "symptoms" of resentment, fear, puzzlement about an altered future that may or may not include them?

3. In any hospital its health professionals, especially physicians and nurses, are, to say the least, protective of their status, recognition, and prerogatives. (And these were two teaching, university-affiliated hospitals!) One does not have to be a semi-sage to say that these professionals would not view the merger with other than deep concern. I do not feel it is necessary to list the questions the merger aroused in their minds.

4. From my perspective the group that would feel the most concern would also be the largest: the diverse non- or semi-professionals who are the least powerful, the most expendable, the least educated or skilled. Here, again, it is not necessary to list what went through their minds when they learned of the merger.

The two institutions were hospitals, but they had two different cultures and traditions. That they were similar in many ways goes without saying, but just as two elementary schools, or two universities, or two families have some common characteristics, they each have a distinctive feel, "soul," ambience, and self-definition. As I said earlier, the hospital on whose advisory committee I served regarded itself and was so regarded by others (locally and nationally) as distinctive, bordering on unique. This, I should hasten to add, is no put-down of the other hospital but rather is a way of saying that they were "psychologically" two different settings. In my 1972 book, I emphasized that the leader gathers around him or her a "core group" which, however devoted to the stated purposes of the new setting, is composed of different *individuals, personalities, and personal-professional experience.* These differences inevitably loom larger in practical import after the creation of the setting than before. That is old hat to people who marry and who may have known each other, or even have lived with each other, for a considerable time before marriage. Merging two cultures is, of course, exponentially more complicated. I felt safe in assuming that each hospital knew itself in a way it did not and could not know the other.

What were the stated purposes of the merger? Those purposes were not easy to come by, in part because the immediate purpose was so obvious: In a quickly changing health care scene in which economic competition from insurance companies and HMOs was approaching cutthroat intensity, the merging of two highly regarded hospitals made the survival of each far more likely at the level and with the quality consistent with past performance. I knew that in the preceding year "my" hospital had explored the possibility of a merger with at least one other major hospital but that discussion proved fruitless for reasons never made clear to me. It was not a good "match"; the problems were too many and thorny. The merger with the nearby hospital apparently was less fraught with predictable difficulties because the major strengths of each were somewhat different, each could add to the strengths of the other, each would become better and stronger. There was another purpose and that was that each hospital would be minimally impacted, its "character" would not change except minimally, i.e., in relatively unimportant ways (unspecified).

It would be unfair to say that the leader of the hospital conveyed the impression to us that the merger would not be beset by thorny problems. But it is not unfair to say that he truly felt that those problems would not be disruptive, that there was a degree of goodwill and clarity of understanding that would overcome what difficulties would be encountered. He expressed no reservations. Given what I have written about what frail reeds goodwill, good intentions, and enthusiasm-optimism are as insurance in the creation of a setting, my skepticism was not assuaged. It is insurance, but it is of the *short-term* variety.

It was during the discussion that the obvious dawned on me: The public announcement of the merger had already introduced a new dynamic in the cultures of the two hospitals. Indeed, rumors of the proposed merger had surfaced before the final decision had been made. What the formal announcement did was galvanize everyone to confront and think about a new future which conceivably would alter plans, hopes, ambitions, working conditions—let alone the possibility that you will not be in that institutional future. I do not say that on the basis of any interviewing I or anyone else did but rather as a glimpse of the obvious for which no interviewing is necessary. What I say is one thing, what those who are managing the merger *need to know* in a very concrete way is quite another thing. There was no indication that any special efforts were being made to sample and respond to the concerns and questions, to give people the feeling that those concerns and questions were important, expected, and would be dealt with. In this instance I must emphasize that the rumors and then the announcement had introduced a new dynamic in both hospitals the consequences of which may be minimal or large. The point is that you must not ignore that or a similar dynamic.

65

The merger was one item on the agenda, and the discussion of it provided no answers to almost all of my questions. What it did provide was confirmation of two features of the process of the creation of other settings. The first is that the creators have no guiding, systematic conception or framework that acts as a control over the major variables in thinking and action which can contribute to failure or cause the setting to take a direction at variance with its stated purposes, i.e., the setting survives but it is not the setting that was envisioned. For example, builders of bridges have a detailed conception of how to build the structure so that it will achieve its intended purposes and will not endanger the lives of people who construct or use it. Indeed, the builders know how to calculate the predictable stresses to which the bridge will be subjected. The number of cars it can hold, the range of weather conditions at the site, the durability of materials. Having made those calculations they add a safety factor to deal with stresses discernibly beyond "normal" or predicable conditions, i.e., they know from the history of bridge building that you have to plan for usual *and* unusual conditions. Similarly, no surgeon in the two hospitals operates on the assumption that he or she will not have to alter the procedures he or she will employ. They have learned—it is central to their cognitive map of the human body—that what was usual in past similar cases may or may not be usual with the next patient. In fact, the operation has associated with it a number of safety factors "just in case." Safety factors are essentially preventive in nature.

The creators of settings—certainly in the case of the hospital merger—do not have an articulate guide, map, or conception of what they have undertaken. It is not that they are flying blind, so to speak. That would be an unwarranted assertion. It is rather that they are unaware that they have not identified (a) the major aspects of the process that result in errors of omission and commission, (b) the kinds of actions that might or can reduce those errors, and (c) the resources of time and personnel which those actions require. It is (c) which, in the case of the hospital merger, confirmed what I said about time perspective in the creation of settings, i.e., a very unrealistic time perspective that derives from an egregious underestimation of the complexity and demands of the process. No one seeks to create a setting in a way that will defeat its purposes. But if your conception of the process is incomplete or superficial, you may achieve wisdom long after you can rectify your errors of omission or commission. "If only I had known this, or done that, or I had allowed myself more time"—these are the frequent, private reflections of almost all leaders of new settings I have known. One such person put it this way: "My enthusiasm for what we wanted to do was so strong and compelling that I was totally insensitive to the fact that I was operating according to a self-constructed time schedule that I know now was nonsensical and blotted out any sensitivity I had to warning signs that all was not going smoothly." But no less important than internal pressures to press ahead are external pressures, ranging from the requirements of funding sources to present a calendar-driven schedule to which you are expected to adhere, to the fact that the new setting can be expected to be subject to pressures either from diverse sources in the larger institution in which it will be embedded or from the many organizations in the geographical area who do not perceive the new setting in neutral terms, i.e., they may see themselves, directly or indirectly, now or later, as being affected by the new settings. The leaders of new settings so tend to rivet in thought and action on that setting that they pay little attention to other external settings. It is as if they divide the world into "in here" and "out there," and it is the former on which their attention rivets. That is why I paid special attention to the "before-the-beginning" phase. It is in that phase that the roles of external forces and vested interests make their appearance, unobtrusively and even nonintrusively, although once the new setting becomes a reality some of those forces and interests may become pressure- and problem-producing.

I said earlier that the merger was not intended to alter in any significant way the culture and character of either hospital.

There would be economic-procedural changes to increase efficiency and the ability to compete, but those changes would not, we were told, dilute the health care, research, and educational performance of either. In fact, it was envisioned that the merger would very likely increase the leadership of both in the medical community; they would be better than and superior to other hospitals and to their own parts.

I regarded the belief that you can introduce economic changes and limit or isolate their impact so that the character of the setting hardly changes to be very problematic—not impossible, but highly unlikely, if only because the immediate stimulus for the merger was an economic one. More correctly, precisely because the economic factor was so obvious and strong, it is not an indulgence of pessimism to say that economic pressures have a dynamic hard to contain. And, experience indicates, when those pressures do not readily have their intended financial consequences, the scope and impact of those pressures tend to enlarge. I believe the president of the hospital knew that. But I also believe that his enthusiasm for the merger caused him to misevaluate that possibility. What if the economic changes do not achieve their intended purpose? I tried to pose that question, but given the constraints of time and the agenda the question never got answered. What was behind that question was another one: If the desired economic benefits were not forthcoming, was there agreement that additional specified economic measures would have to be taken which, however unpalatable, would have demonstrable, percolating noneconomic consequences? If there were no discussion and agreement on that possibility, there was trouble ahead.

From what I have said the reader would be quite justified in feeling that I have described a problem and process that are bewilderingly complex and beset with potholes which convince you that if given the opportunity to create a new setting, you would pass up the opportunity. Bear in mind that in this chapter I have been discussing the merger of two large, complex organizations which compared to two people entering

68

marriage is a difference that does make a difference. But we have to ask why so many marriages fail. Granted that mergers and marriages are vastly different in scale, but that does not mean that what makes for success or failure in marriage is in theory and practice irrelevant to success or failure of mergers. I believe that the variables are identical, however different they are in scale and context.

What I have just said and described reflects what went through my mind at the time of the advisory committee meeting in which we were informed of the coming merger of the two hospitals. As to what would be the developmental dynamics of the merger I had only hunches, gloomy ones. I can assure the reader that I do not have a depressive personality. But I do have what I call a "what if" tendency in regard to living in a world I do not, cannot control and which can be predictably unpredictable. What will I do if this or that happens? I have no trouble whatever imagining scads of this or that and for each I try to come up with scenarios of how to deal with the what ifs. My what if tendency has its positive and negative features. The negative is that I take very little for granted: Trouble is not around the corner, it is coming down the street I am on. The positive aspect is that I develop scenarios for the what ifs, for the "just in case" occasions. I am being candidly personal here in order to make the point that creating and sustaining a new setting is not for everyone motivated to create a new setting, just as mountain climbing is not for everyone even if he or she has the motivation and physical strength to engage in that endeavor. We are used to hearing that the devil is in the details. In the case of planning to create and sustain a new setting the details are many, thorny, and for the most part predictable, but only if your stance takes seriously what we know about human relationships, frailties, and the tendency to oversimplify what may lie ahead.

My gloomy hunches were more than confirmed. There were power struggles, recriminations, rebellion, a series of shakeups and changes in leadership, and plummeting morale, much of this reported in the local newspapers. I take no satisfaction whatsoever from confirmation of my gloomy hunches. To be completely candid I did not regard them as hunches. From personal experience and extensive observations, I was ready to bet and give handsome odds that the merger would not accomplish its purposes. Bear in mind that fifty or more percent of all new marriages end in divorce and that an undetermined but significant number of new business ventures—instances of creating new settings—go out of existence or file for bankruptcy.

My pessimism about what charter schools can or will demonstrate will be greeted differently by opponents and proponents of them. That would be unfortunate and unjustified, and ultimately self-defeating for both sides.

CHAPTER 7

VOUCHERS AND SCHOOL CHOICE

The word *education* does not appear in our federal constitution. That was not an oversight. It was taken for granted by the founding fathers that education was the responsibility of parents, the local community, and the state. The federal government had no role in education; it was feared that it could exercise its power and resources to contravene the wishes and values of people in regard to an activity of major importance for the lives of children and the well-being of the country. To people of those days, "That government is best which rules the least" was not empty rhetoric but an expression of how deeply they felt about protecting individual liberty from the excesses of powerful government which made the war for independence necessary. Not until early in the twentieth century did the federal government create an office of education, which was piddling in size and had no power (for all practical purposes) to influence education or to tell or require any state or local community to do anything. That did not change until several years after World War II when it became apparent there was what came to be called the urban crisis.

A colleague of mine, Dr. Samuel Brownell, was the U.S. Commissioner of Education in the early years of the Eisenhower presidency. Dr. Brownell was quite sensitive to the dimensions of the urban problem and its increasing disorganizing and morale-lowering impact on schools. It was obvious to him that neither the cities nor the states had the resources to deal with the problems, and that unless the federal government entered the picture the consequences of inaction would be socially disruptive. It was arranged for Dr. Brownell to present his case for a change in federal policy to President Eisenhower and his cabinet, a fact testifying to the significance attached to such a policy change. Dr. Brownell presented his case, following which the president asked each member of the cabinet to express an opinion. Without exception each member advised against the policy change, although some recognized the gravity of the situation. Finally, President Eisenhower turned to Vice President Nixon for his opinion and he unequivocally supported Dr. Brownell's argument and recommendation. At this point President Eisenhower expressed agreement with both Nixon and Brownell and the wheels were set in motion to develop vehicles for federal intervention. President Eisenhower's decision ushered in a dramatic change in the relationship between schools and the federal government. What must be noted is that it brought in its wake a complexity that was prodromal of future problems. One significance of that action was the impetus it provided for increasing the number and variety of professionals in schools. Especially in our urban areas, the flow of federal funds, a flow that in subsequent years seemed to be more of a torrent, led to such an increase in the size and varieties of educational personnel as to make administration a preoccupation of everyone. Neither before, then, nor now has the management of quick growth been handled well. To those who lived through those days, their experience was made up of optimism about the future and frustration about the increasing and bewildering bureaucratization of schools. The growth in internal complexity brought with it an escalation of power struggles among the diverse professional groupings.

The second external development that played into these internal power dynamics was somewhat more complicated and subtle, at its beginnings at least. There are different but related ways by which one may label the decade or so after World War II. The Age of Psychology, the Age of the Child, and the Age of Mental Health are labels that reflect the heightened awareness and concern of parents about child rearing and education. Those were the years when Spock's book on child rearing was the bible for millions of parents intent on insuring that their children would grow and learn, i.e., take maximum advantage of educational opportunities. Those were also the days when the phrase "to develop the child's potential to the fullest" entered common parlance. Parents became interested in and articulate about learning and schooling as never before. They wanted "good" schools and they fought for them. But in advocating for and supporting increased educational budgets, parents were in no way challenging the responsibility of educators to decide the substance of the educational process. Generally speaking, the community and school personnel saw eye-to-eye about what needed to be done. This was a period when schools enjoyed a rare degree of community support. People today need to be reminded that one of the sources of the militancy of teacher unions in those early decades after World War II was parental support. How could you expect teachers to do a good job with such pitiful compensation? And what that question obscured was the fact that the diverse professional groups in schools, each in its own way, had begun to challenge the educational decision-making process, a process that at its core deals with the allocation of resources. Those challenges, however, were based on the *assumption* that decision making, however the process might be altered, was the responsibility of the *professionals*. The power struggles within the school reinforced the long-standing principle that, in practice, decision making was primarily the responsibility of the professional educator, legal fictions to the contrary notwithstanding. But beginning with the 1954 desegregation decision, helping to set the stage as it did for the "turbulent sixties," the questions of who owns the schools and who should have a voice in determining the *substance* of education came to the fore. And when it came to the fore the core issue was the role of parents and other community groups in educational decision making. That proposed role presented a direct challenge to the power of the school professionals. *That* power struggle, *that* polarization was far more public and violent than the struggles and polarizations among the professionals. Far from community groups viewing school professionals as part of the solution, they came to see them as part of the problem. The polarization continues today, the level of conflict waxing and waning, but always there.

There are several principles undergirding the constitution and one of them is the political principle: If actions and decisions are going to be made which affect the lives of people, those people should have a role or platform by which they can influence those actions and decisions (Sarason 1995). "Taxation without representation is tyranny" was an expression by the colonists of that principle. Needless to say, in our interpersonal, social, working lives outside the political arena we are familiar with that principle: We do not take kindly to the actions and decisions which others take which affect us in some negative way but about which we had no say or role. We may call it a lack of sensitivity or courtesy, or say it is cruel, or whatever, but we resent not to have been in some way involved in the action or decision.

Vouchers and school choice bring to the fore the political principle in the form of this question: Independent of money considerations, does a parent have the right to send her child to a school other than the one he would ordinarily go to because that school for one reason or another is deemed unsatisfactory by the parent? Does the parent have the right to send her child to no school but rather to "homeschool" her child? The answer to both questions is, of course, yes, in the abstract and the concrete; in the concrete, if the parents have the money to pay tuition to attend a private or parochial school or in the case homeschooling can meet reasonable criteria for establishing the conditions of the child's education. (There are more than a million home-schoolers in this country and many more millions in private and parochial schools.) In brief, parents are the ultimate decision makers in these instances and that is legally-constitutionally recognized and sanctioned.

But what if parents cannot afford to take advantage of that right and responsibility? What options do they have if they are dissatisfied with what their child is learning and how he is being treated in his public school? Up until about ten years ago these parents had only one option: to seek to get the school to change the child's classroom or, depending on the parent's complaint, to change what the parent considered to be an unsatisfactory, or unhealthy, or dangerous environment. Many inner-city parents—many parents in blue-collar neighborhoods—felt too personally inadequate or inferior to tangle with school personnel "far above them" in education, fluency, and authority even to go to the school with their grievances. They, so to speak, adopted a grin-and-bear-it stance or an attitude conveyed in the "go fight city hall" stance. I say that because for a decade I and my colleagues worked in these schools (many of them far less than adequate by conventional criteria) and we were struck by how rare it was for a parent to come to the school with a complaint. That did surprise school personnel who regarded these parents as uninterested in their children's education. It did not take us long to discover that their judgment was a myth. Far from being uninterested, parents felt impotent and intimidated by school personnel who regarded them as ignorant and irresponsible. It was an example of the negative self-fulfilling prophecy: You start with the belief that a person is incapable, you treat that person as if he or she is incapable, and you end up proving you were right in the first place. Inner-city parents, we found, were victims of the same fallacy: They started with the belief that school personnel would be unreceptive to their complaints, so they did nothing, and then when the situation of the child deteriorated, they were confirmed in their belief that school personnel did not know how to handle students, and that complaining about it was an exercise in futility. These negative, self-fulfilling dynamics are frequent in suburban schools but with an ironic twist: The more educated the parents, the less fearful they are to express their complaints loud and clear; school personnel regard them as arrogant complainers, their interactions can be stormy, and they each regard the other in negative, disrespectful ways.

75

Because what I have said above is crucial to what I shall discuss later, let me present an example of legislation that affected every school in the country before vouchers or school choice (they are *not* the same) appeared in the educational scene.

Early in the fifties a small group of parents of retarded children met to form the National Association for Retarded Children. Like so many parents of these children, they were more than fed up with the lack of interest of schools in providing educational programs for their children. What programs existed could accommodate a fraction of these children and the programs were isolated from everything and everyone else in the school. Although the number of children who needed and could benefit from an educational program was very large, the number of classrooms was piddling. Even so, the criteria for admission to a program insured that those who would be accepted would be those who would not place a burden on their teachers or existing resources. If a child was not selected, the parent was informed and that was the end of that. Children with associated physical or sensory handicaps stood no chance of being accepted. There was no appeal process. The parent had two options: continue to care and train the child as best she could at home or place the child in a state institution which was usually in the middle of rural nowhere and which consisted of old, very large, congregate buildings containing unconscionably more children than they had originally been planned for. They were warehouses, human ones. However interesting the story is, it is beyond my purpose to explain how in the next decade or so the NARC became one of the most effective lobbyists in state legislatures to require schools to increase access of their children to schools and improve existing programs many of which were somewhat better than baby-sitting affairs. At the end of the sixties Massachusetts passed legislation the NARC had proposed; other states began to follow, although most did not. Finally, in 1975 Congress passed Public Law 94-142, the so-called mainstreaming law, which mandated that schools had to develop programs for all handicapped children regardless of the sources of their handicap: mental, neurological, sensory, physical. There were no ifs or buts. Schools were educational institutions and they had no right to deny access on the basis of handicap. Parents and children were citizens which meant that schools no longer could make unilateral decisions affecting children without parents participating in the decision-making process. The National Association for Retarded Children changed its name to the National Association for Retarded *Citizens*. Citizens had rights which had to be recognized and respected.

I began my career in the field of mental retardation in 1942 and never in a million years would I have predicted the 1975 legislation. In fact my first job was in a new state institution for the mentally retarded; it would not surprise me if I learned that this institution was the first new one in the twentieth century. I know that many of the then-existing institutions were built in the nineteenth century, which was true in Connecticut. What astounded me about the 1975 legislation was the section on the role of parents in decision making about their children. It was a role putting flesh on the bones of the political principle. I arranged a meeting with the chief lobbyist for the legislation. It turned out that he had drafted what he called the civil rights section, which consisted of the following:

1. If the child needed special education services the school had to so inform the parent.

2. There would then be a case conference at which the parent had to be present.

3. Whatever the program proposed for the child, it could not be implemented unless the parent was in agreement.

4. The child could not, should not, be segregated from the rest of the school. It was the obligation of the school to mainstream the child to the fullest extent. In the words of the law, the child should be placed in the least restrictive environment.

5. If the parent does not agree with the proposed program, she can take advantage of an appeal process that goes beyond the local school system.

There are two features of the legislation the importance of which cannot be overestimated. The first is that it mandates a process which rivets on the individual child for the purpose of tailoring a program that takes into account that child's needs, problems, assets, and deficits. There is no such mandate for other students. The second feature is that parents are given a role and influence they never were accorded before; such a formal mandate was not applicable to parents of "regular" students.

What is the significance of the history of the landmark mainstreaming legislation for school choice and vouchers? The answer is identical to the answer in regard to charter schools: Schools and school systems were insensitive to and ignored the grievances and resentments of parents; they lacked the initiative, imagination, and courage to devise departures from tradition; they were reactive and not proactive. I am not scapegoating school personnel, as if to say they *willed* the problems with which they came to be confronted. The fact is that the post-World War II-era schools, like every other major traditional institution, were late in *recognizing* and *responding to* the social upheavals that were direct or indirect consequences of World War II. It is said that war changes everyone and everything. That was certainly true for World War II.

One of the ways schools, by no means all, responded was to embrace the concept of school choice, which in the abstract meant that parents could request that their children be enrolled in school *x* rather than the one he or she would ordinarily attend in *that* city. At the same time that school choice was gaining currency, some school systems developed magnet schools which would enlarge the choice parents could explore. In effect, school systems were becoming more responsive and flexible to parental perspectives.

What were the predictable problems school choice would present to schools and parents? From the standpoint of the school system the most obvious problem derived from the fact that the bulk of existing schools were already crowded and would be unable to enroll other than a few transfers from other schools. On the justified assumption that parents would choose schools they heard were "good" schools, those schools could accommodate only a small number of transfers, thus disappointing a fair number of parents; for these parents school choice was no choice. I was involved with two new magnet schools, one a middle and the other a high school, both in a large city. In the first year both schools enrolled less than the number of students that they could accommodate. By the beginning of the second year it was a different story: They were flooded by parents seeking to enroll their children. Over several years they became overcrowded and whatever program quality and respect for student individuality they previously had sought and, in part at least, accomplished were diluted, not extinguished but noticeably, predictably less in evidence.

Another predictable problem was how school principals viewed school choice, a problem hardly discussed in the school choice literature. Those principals who had cause to believe that their schools were not highly regarded, were "troubled" schools, feared they would lose their "best" students, the "creaming" phenomenon, and as a result their troubled schools would become more troubled, morale would deteriorate, making it more difficult to improve educational outcomes. And in some inner-city schools there were principals who never informed parents that they had a choice or who sought to dissuade parents from transferring their children. But what about the principals of the schools from which students would come? Would principals likely agree to transfer children the school would like to get rid of? Also, there were principals concerned that some parents might be complainers who would expect or demand too much of the school to which they sought to transfer their child. I bring up these fears and expectations to make the point that any non-cosmetic educational reform inevitably—and I use that word advisedly— encounters obstacles deriving from the complex culture of schools and school systems. I cannot say how often decisions about school choice undermined the purposes of school choice. All I can say is that those obstacles are predictable and were operative. Parents can choose, but in subtle and non-subtle ways features of the culture of school systems can facilitate or defeat the choice or, more likely, complicate matters for parents.

Depending on the size of the city, there is another predictable problem: transportation. What if the city permits school choice but is unable or unwilling to provide transportation in instances where the school a parent chooses is, so to speak, far from being around the corner? That, of course, is especially a problem for parents whose children are in elementary and middle schools. If the parents have a car and at least one of the parents has the time to transport the child to and from the school, there is no problem. But what if the parents do not have a car, or only one car which one of them uses for work and the work schedule conflicts with the opening and end of the school day? And living as we are at a time when both parents work and they have only one car, transporting the child to the school of parental choice can amount to no choice at all.

Illuminating the bedrock importance of practical consideration in accomplishing the purposes of school choice is a report by Rothstein (2001) of Seattle's program, which he describes as "voucherizing" school choice because transferring students will come with funds over and beyond the per capita expenditure for every Seattle student. That feature is absent (to my knowledge) in all other school choice programs. Rothstein writes:

> Federal Title I money already provides extra resources to the most needy schools. But because it usually operates only where poverty is concentrated and barriers to learning are greater, Title I is no incentive for middle-class schools to recruit low-income pupils in manageable numbers. Some advocates say Title I money should follow students even if they attend middle-class schools. The idea

has merit, but would spread limited federal dollars too thinly.

So Seattle's idea of "voucherizing" regular expenditures is a smart move. Pupils with greater needs—because of poverty, limited English or disability—bring more regular district money. Unfortunately, however, the plan is more show than substance; the differentials are too small to make a difference. A low-income elementary pupil brings only $259 in extra resources. If the increments were bigger, schools enrolling such students could offer more attractive programs to both middle-class and low-income parents.

Seattle's white middle class mostly lives north of downtown; lower-income blacks mostly live to the south. If differential bonuses were greater, integration might occur. Some southside schools might be so awash in money, they could create superior programs to attract middle-class pupils. Some northside schools might want to pad budgets by recruiting poorer children.

This does not now happen. Hay Elementary School just north of downtown, for instance, has no reason to recruit low-income students. Their vouchers do not bring enough added money to pay for help such pupils need.

Ironically, Rothstein's conclusion that the Seattle program is more "show than substance" is one with which the Seattle superintendent of schools seems to agree. He said that more important than extra funds are the flexibility and imagination of principals to devise new and better programs. I have to conclude that the superintendent expects little from the school choice program. That, of course, begs the question: What is he doing to reform schools that (a) are educationally weak or (b) will reduce the pressures for a school choice program likely to accomplish little, or (c) both? One of the arguments in favor of school choice is that it will act as a competitive spur to educationally below-average schools. Well, if you have little faith that will occur, you are back to square one: How do you improve schools generally? How do you select and support principals who can transform their schools? Are the superintendent and the board of education prepared to support transformations that predictably will be, for a time at least, destabilizing, even explosive? Or is it that the top leadership of the system, plus the board of education, are part of the problem and not the solution? Is it possible—and I would say likely—that these layers of authority are vastly underestimating the readiness of the community to embrace reforms which are more credibly substance and not show?

It is old hat among organizational consultants to private sector corporations that they are brought in by the top leadership who proceed to tell them where the sources of the corporation's troubles are. Invariably, they do not describe themselves as a source but rather identify layers of staff below them as the major culprits. Having been an organizational consultant to school systems, I have observed the same sort of blame assignment. The board of education is critical of the superintendent, who is critical of his or her administrative staff, who is critical of teachers. The one thing they tend to agree on is that parents and the larger community hamstring school personnel—by policies and niggardly funding—from improving schools. They are unaware that there are schools which were grossly inadequate but were transformed by school personnel and parents to an extent never expected. *Some of those schools were in the inner city.* I suggest the reader read a book by Dr. Paul Heckman and teacher associates titled *The Courage to Change* (1995), and the book *Children of the Dust Bowl* (Stanley 1992). The latter book is a most engrossing account of what can be created with practically no funds but with a great deal of courage, creativity, and a redefinition of resources.

Advocacy for school change is based on more than the political principle. It is based also on the perceived need to stimulate the motivating spirit of competition among schools in the school system. That purpose has been an issue long before school choice came onto the scene and it was about merit pay. Indeed, in the April 2001 negotiations between the New York City Teacher Union and the city political leadership, the union opposed merit pay increases for *individual* teachers whose students show better than expected gains on achievement tests. The assumption is that merit pay increase to individual teachers will spur other teachers to improve the performance of their students and if they cannot to suffer the pain of being perceived as inadequate and, perhaps, decide to leave the field. The union was opposed on several grounds. It would cause enmity among teachers in the school. Those who decide who gets or does not get a merit pay increase are not unbiased individuals inoculated against playing favorites. Principals have the obligation to play an active role to help teachers become better teachers. Finally, the performance of a teacher's students may not be what one expected but that teacher contributed to the school in ways not reflected in test scores. Therefore, and for the first time ever, the union proposed that if the *overall* performance of the students in that school is better than expected, then *all* personnel in the school should be given a merit pay increase. The counterargument to the union proposal was that utilizing the criterion of overall performance may obscure the fact that a number of teachers contributed to that average and that less productive teachers have no reason to change their outlook and practices; what will spur them to compete, to improve? Why reward them with a merit pay increase they have not earned?

In the article on the negotiations in the *New York Times* on May 4, 2001, is the following paragraph:

> Education experts said the union's signal that it might accept some form of performance-based pay, after months of denouncing Mr. Giuliani's merit pay plan, could end the negotiating stalemate of months and serve as the basis of a deal. This week, during a delicate time in the contract talks, the union's newspaper published a full page about schoolwide incentive pay, generally praising the idea and, in particular, a pilot schoolwide incentive pay program that the union has accepted for two school districts in Brooklyn (S. Greenhouse).

That paragraph raises this question: How is the pilot program in the two Brooklyn schools being evaluated? Will that program provide us data, not subjective opinion, by which to judge the arguments of those with very different opinions about competition? As best I have been able to determine, the pilot program will end up in a way requiring no one to change their minds about their positions. But that is an old story about educational policy, implementation, and findings.

That teachers should be rewarded for meritorious performance is, in my opinion, indisputable, a glimpse of the obvious, just as I similarly regard the parental role in school choice. An educational policy is just that: a verbal statement of intent and goal that is based *presumably* on a knowledge of and sensitivity to the nature of the social system that policy intends to change. I italicize "presumably" because schools and school systems are very complicated, interacting organizations composed of groups with different outlooks, power, vested interests, and values. To deny that is to deny the obvious. To expect that a non-cosmetic policy change can be mandated for an entire system and will not encounter major obstacles—especially if the policy involves money, power, and changes in long-standing traditions—is sheer folly. But realistically to assess those obstacles does not justify inaction and it certainly does not justify proceeding in ways from which we will learn nothing about the validity of the assumptions on which the policy is based. In earlier pages of this book I said that in the educational arena we do not have the spirit or tradition of a Federal Drug Administration which essentially says: "Before you can make available to people generally your new drug or medical procedure, you will be required to submit pilot studies and evaluations demonstrating that your initial hopes and claims have an acceptable degree of validity." No one criticizes that spirit and tradition. But when it comes to educational policy intended to affect an entire system, no thought is given to the question: How can we do a circumscribed trial run on the basis of which we can make an informed judgment about whether or how to proceed further? That is why I was pleasantly surprised to learn that the New York Board of Education supported two schools to pilot in regard to the merit pay controversy. But, as I have said, the evaluation of that effort will not provide credible evidences.

How is school choice being evaluated? That policy is intended not only to improve the educational experience and outcomes of students whose parents take advantage of school choice but also to spur schools to improve, to compete, in order that they do not lose students. Whatever evidence we have about school choice, and there is very little evidence, is fragmentary and, to say the least, not compelling.

In Rothstein's article on the Seattle school choice plan, he correctly says that the extra two to three hundred dollars a student will bring to the school his parents choose is clearly too small to stimulate interest in that school to recruit that student. But what if that small sum were tripled or quadrupled? Would that increase the school's interest? It is my opinion, and it is no more than an opinion, that it would have little effect. I lived through the period when Project Concern was devised, which made it possible for a small number of inner-city students to be bused to attend suburban schools. It was essentially a school choice plan, a kind of voucher but without money attached to it. The suburban schools did not embrace Project Concern warmly. That was at a time of racial conflict and the recognition that inner-city schools were antieducational for students. Not all suburban districts chose to participate even though no single suburban school would have more than a few bused students. With each passing year the participating schools were less willing to continue and it did not take long for Project Concern to become a footnote in the history of educational reform. I know of only one Project Concern program that was relatively carefully evaluated and it contains credible evidence that the bused students in Hartford, Connecticut, showed academic gains. I came to know Dr. Thomas Mahan, the director of that program, and I attributed the academic gains to the quality and scope of his leadership. He had anticipated what the problems would be (and were) and he dealt with them so that problems did not become crises. But when he left Hartford, the project went downhill and was terminated. The program was a success without money and a failure when committed, knowledgeable, street-smart leadership left the scene. Dr. Mahan, who had been a teacher and principal, knew the culture of schools and that suffused his relationships with everyone.

Vouchers allow parents school choice but in addition come with funds they can use to enroll their children in a school which may be private, parochial, or another public school outside the boundaries of the city in which the parents reside and, therefore, requiring a tuition fee. Clearly, vouchers are intended for families who do not possess the means to send their children to these schools; they cannot participate freely in the educational "market," their local school system has a "monopoly" in the local market. If that school system allows school choice, it is a restricted choice for poor parents, unlike more affluent parents, who in principle confront no restrictions on school choice. It is not an accident that advocates—certainly the most articulate ones—use economic concepts like monopoly and the market to justify their proposals, saying that just as monopolies have a negative effect on consumers, a free market has a positive one because it spurs competition, increases quality of product, keeps prices in check, and over time reduces prices—for these reasons a free market in education would have similar consequences. Failing public schools and school systems would be confronted with the "shape up or ship out" option: improve and be competitive or you will be out of business, just as many businesses disappear each year because they were not competitive.

Needless to say, many people and almost all (if not all!) school personnel view the rationale for vouchers as a direct assault on the American public school tradition and system. But the voucher proponents say it is not an assault, that there are "good" public schools who will be able to compete and survive, although many will not: How can you justify supporting schools whose track record is scandalously inimical to the future of children, which is the case with so many urban schools in which they are trapped?

Most people have an almost instinctively negative response to vouchers, seeing them as vehicles that will make educationally bad schools worse; that public schools will not be competing on a fair or equal playing field; that the number of "good" or the "best" students in public schools will decrease if not plummet; that the large number of students with special needs or handicaps will rarely be accepted in many private or parochial systems; that in the case of parochial schools the separation between church and state will be increasingly narrowed; that private and parochial schools will seek to recruit students less because they want them and more because they need the funds that will accompany them; that in the history of the American free market there have been countless instances where the pressures of the "bottom line," the need to be profitable, has had unfortunate, or sleazy, immoral, asocial consequences; the free market is not noted for its ethical, self-sacrificing tendencies; that the free market, precisely because it is a competitive one, has led to monopolies, megamergers, and restriction of consumer choice.

In his presidential campaign and in numerous occasions afterward, President George W. Bush made clear his advocacy of vouchers. As I write these words it appears that he will not submit a concrete proposal because, being a good politician, he recognizes the strength of the opposition to vouchers and, besides, budget considerations rule out such a proposal. Unlike school choice, which has gained currency in many urban school districts, it is unlikely that vouchers will gain currency in the next few years if only because they engender both anxiety about and opposition to the prospect of dramatically altering public education as we have known it. But let us not forget that that type of opposition also greeted the earliest proposals for school choice and charter schools. Why, then, was that opposition overcome? By far the most important reason was the *lack of evidence* that despite all efforts to improve student performance and outcomes the results have been disappointing, and in the case of urban schools they have been *depressing*. Therefore, to assume that the current opposition to vouchers signals what will be their fate one or two decades from now is to *ignore* history. Whether or not vouchers will gain currency will depend on the *degree* to which efforts at reform, like charter schools and school choice, higher standards and accountability, and changes in the selection and preparation of school personnel will have their intended effects. If they do not, we can expect that vouchers will gain far more support than they now have, even from those who today oppose them. There is truth to Santayana's caveat that those who ignore history are doomed to repeat it. Let me give an example monumentally relevant to vouchers.

The largest, most ambitious, most successful educational voucher program ever devised in any country was put into place in the United States immediately after World War II. I refer to the GI Bill of Rights for millions of war veterans whose lives had been mammothly disrupted by their induction into the armed services. Here is what the GI Bill permitted and supported:

1. Tuition fees for any program—undergraduate, graduate, professional, vocational—for which the veteran applied and was selected. Where and why the veteran selected a program was solely determined by the veteran.

2. The books (and lab fees) the veterans would be required to purchase for study would be paid for by the federal government.

3. The veteran would receive a monthly living allowance which would vary depending on whether he or she was married and had children.

4. At very little cost the veteran was given a life insurance policy and, in addition, could purchase a home with a mortgage bearing a very low rate of interest.

The GI Bill made it possible for millions of veterans to receive an education they had never dreamed about. Keep in mind that World War II was preceded by the Great Depression during which the unemployment rate reached twenty percent of all adults. For many of these veterans the fantasy of going to college was just that: fantasy. So was the fantasy of owning a home.

It is hard to overestimate how the lives of most veterans were literally transformed by the GI Bill. "Do you want an education of your choice? If you find an educational institution of your choice whose criteria for enrollment you can meet, a grateful society will underwrite it." That was the message of the GI Bill. It was an unbridled voucher program that not only changed the size of the "educational market" but the nature of our society as well. I have been in the higher education arena since the end of World War II and during that time I never met anyone who took advantage of the GI Bill who did not express bottomless gratitude for what it enabled him or her to experience and become. I never met anyone in any field—I refer to those who were *not* veterans but were parents or friends of GIs, or later colleagues of GIs—who voiced any criticism of the program. In a program on C-Span in early 2001 the historian Stephen Ambrose ventured the opinion that the GI Bill was the single most encompassing, society-transforming, successful piece of legislation ever to be enacted by the federal government. I agree.

Before President Bush II advocated for school vouchers, his father, President Bush I, called for vouchers and went on to say that he favored a GI Bill of Rights for children, recalling as he did, by virtue of having been a veteran, what the GI Bill had meant to veterans of his generation. But what he sketched in his brief remarks made a mockery of the comparison because, if memory serves me correctly, he called for a voucher worth somewhere between $1,500 and $2,000. He clearly did not know (I am being charitable here) what the tuition is in private schools, many parochial schools, or what some public schools charge parents who do not live in their community. He also seemed unaware that after World War II practically every college and university welcomed the veterans regardless of who they were or where they came from, despite the fact that by doing so these institutions would confront an array of administrative, housing, and personal problems. That is far from the case today in the private and parochial school arena, who at best could enroll a piddling number of new students, aware as these institutions are that the size and the quality of programs are their strengths, and they will understandably be resistant to what they consider to be threats to their educational strengths. Nor did President Bush I (or II) say anything about the size of the voucher for urban school families who do not have the means to make up for what the voucher does not pay. Voucher advocates can only resort to their treasured assumption that in a free, minimally regulated market, vouchers will be the competition-stimulating factor for imaginative entrepreneurs to create schools appropriate to the means of what parents can pay.

The GI Bill was not a financial token gesture. First, it was adequate (neither piddling nor luxurious) to stimulate veterans to redirect their education to their interests and hopes. Second, it was a stimulus to higher education to enroll veterans without fear of financial loss or having to compromise standards. Third, it would (and did) stimulate many colleges and universities to improve their programs and to compete more effectively for students.

The GI Bill was the right program at the right time for the veteran population. What would be the right voucher program for schoolchildren? What we get from voucher advocates are phrases, labels, and theories centering around economic concepts like the free market, competition, accountability, and the wonders of entrepreneurialism. We are given nothing that tells us what the predictable problems will be in light of all we have learned about schools, educational reform, the complexity and frailties of human behavior, and the centrality of people's concern for their psychological and fiscal bottom lines. We are used to hearing that the devil is in the details. To a truly surprising extent the GI Bill dealt with the details. The voucher proponents have provided us with no details.

I have not said what I have as a way of dismissing or refuting the concept of vouchers. I was a proponent of the concept of charter schools until I became aware of the details of the way they were being created and implemented. In the case of school vouchers I will not take a pro or con stance until I am given the details where devils reside. Of one thing I am certain: Should voucher proponents come to the realization about how much money it will cost to make it possible for parents of little or modest means to use and benefit from vouchers, the proponents will lose their enthusiasm. The GI Bill was not cheap but it was successful. A realistic school voucher program will not be cheap. I seriously doubt that proponents are prepared for that eventuality.

When the readers of this book hear what voucher proponents say, they should try to refrain from a pro or con stance and instead ask about the details—the "Where's the beef" stance—the nitty-gritty details, like who will benefit most and least from such a policy. In what ways does the policy deal with the predictable problem of how to make an uneven playing field more even? Have we learned nothing from a Medicare program which was justified by assessments and costs which turned out to be disastrously optimistic, the scope of benefits was scaled back, and the quality of nursing home care went steadily downhill as entrepreneurs were faced with bottom lines written in red ink? Need I say anything about the vaunted efficiencies in cost and quality we were told would flow from an HMO system?

The purpose of this book was to indicate and discuss questions we should ask about what we need to know in passing judgment about the accomplishments of charter schools, school choice, and voucher programs. I deliberately stayed away from technical and theoretical issues of which there are many. I emphasized questions of obvious practical import, the sort of hands-on questions asked about new, much-heralded reforms of a controversial nature. They are questions which may not have been obvious to readers but, I assumed, would very quickly be considered as obvious when I posed those questions in these pages. What frequently happens when we see the obvious is that the obvious is no simple affair from the standpoint of explaining. For example, take what I have described elsewhere, the 5-2 regularity: For five days of the week, schools are densely populated places, followed by two days when they are devoid of people. Why not 4-3, 6-1, or 2-5? It is obvious that there can be more than one regularity for school attendance. So when you are asked why the 5-2 regularity is universal in America, you are very likely not to have a ready answer. There are people who answer by saying that the 5-2 regularity must have been determined on the basis of an educational rationale or theory, which claimed that that regularity was most conducive to learning. If you then start reading the history of education in this country, you find that the 5-2 regularity had precious little to do with an educational rationale and a great deal to do with national history and culture. Our history and culture is complicated, very complicated. Our schools did not develop as they did because of an educational rationale which purported to show that the 5-2 regularity was most effective in stimulating and sustaining learning. The obvious is one thing, explaining and justifying it is another thing.

Initially, I planned that this would be the last chapter. But as I started writing, a nagging thought kept intruding and it took the form of a question. Since any educational reform explicitly seeks to improve and sustain learning, how clear is the reform about the nature of the learning process and experience? It is obvious that schools are contexts of learning. But there is learning and there is learning. What do we want the internal and external features of learning to accomplish and demonstrate? What consequences would satisfy or dissatisfy us? What interferes with or capitalizes on the learning process and experience? Those are questions that have a very long controversial history. However, it is not a history we can ignore. Even when we ignore, as is so often the case, we are unaware that we proceed as if we are clear about what we understand to be the nature of learning and why our understanding is "better" than another person's understanding.

It was these types of questions which forced me to write the next and final chapter. If it is obvious that charter schools and vouchers, like any other educational reform, seek to change, improve, and sustain learning, I would be shortchanging the reader if I said nothing about the concept of learning. To say little or nothing is tantamount to equating educational reform to shadowboxing. At the very least, the next chapter reveals a major source of my pessimism about what charter schools and vouchers will demonstrate.

CHAPTER 8

CONTEXTS OF PRODUCTIVE
AND UNPRODUCTIVE LEARNING

I have tried in this book to raise issues and ask questions about charter schools, vouchers, and school choice. I have not attempted to convince opponents and proponents to change their opinions. What I have tried to do is to indicate that these policies are not as simple as they appear, that they ignore or gloss over issues that explain why educational reform has fallen so short of its mark. Granted that these policies are relatively new, that does not mean that past reform efforts are irrelevant to how we think about these policies. The fact is that these new policies are but new expressions of the goals of past efforts. For one thing, like past efforts, the new policies are a response to the recognition that, generally speaking, our schools are disappointing in their educational outcomes; more than disappointing, they appear to have been intractable to change. For another thing, like past non-cosmetic changes, these new policies explicitly require changes in the accustomed ways schools are what they are. No reform effort, past or present, disguises its goal that changes have to take place if the quality of outcomes is to improve. That is a statement to which it is easy to nod assent but as the history of educational reform documents, changing a complicated institution like a school or school system is horrendously difficult and it has been by no means clear why that has been the case. Different reformers come to different conclusions, leaving the public and elected officials bewildered and sympathetic to more radical and even semipunitive policies. So, for example, many states have criticized school personnel for not maintaining high academic standards, for expecting too little of students, for promoting them when they do not deserve promotion, and for not rigorously using tests on the basis of which schools and their personnel can be held accountable. School personnel are not in doubt that they are being blamed for poor outcomes. They are, they feel, not only being blamed but in danger of being victims of a "shape up or ship out" policy. And when they see how discussion of charter schools and vouchers is implicitly and explicitly critical of school personnel, it is understandable if they feel threatened and scapegoated. Tests have been given such importance in the lives of school personnel, students, and parents that there is an increase of reports in the mass media of the adverse consequences of "teaching to the test." In Scarsdale, New York, one of the most affluent communities in America, parents organized a protest to the state department of education, which includes the statement that they would keep their students home on the day the tests were to be given. In the *New York Times* there is an article on cheating scandals in at least six states on new state-mandated tests. And tomorrow (June 11, 2001) teachers in New Haven, Connecticut are staging a protest before the board of education to call attention to how "teaching to the test" is watering down and narrowing what students are learning. None of this should be surprising. Indeed it was predictable. When people, in this case students and school personnel, find themselves in a situation where test performance will influence lives in adverse ways, you do not have to be a psychological expert to predict that *some* people will cheat, especially when they feel the tests are unfair for one or another reason. I am not *condoning* cheating, I am trying to *understand* it because if the *New York Times* report turns out to be the tip of an iceberg, those who set the standards and approved the tests should be obligated to explain on what *basis* they set the standards and approved the tests. Please note that when in some states the analysis of test scores indicated that many students (in the thousands) would not be promoted or graduated, they extended the number of years for the consequences of the shape up or ship out policy to go into effect. It is a mess—educationally, morally, politically, and psychologically—from which, I fear, we will continue to ignore what I consider to be the most basic and yet unanswered question. I will illustrate what I mean by presenting my clinical experience with two young boys, two of my diagnostic errors I discuss in an earlier publication. I can assure the reader that I have made more than two errors. But those errors forced me to a conclusion which dramatically influenced how I came to understand why educational reform would be minimal in its consequences. That understanding did not come quickly. I resisted it. I had a lot to unlearn.

CASE 1

I was in 1942 the psychologist in a spanking-new state training school for mentally retarded individuals. There were certain times during the week when "children" could be admitted to the Southbury Training School. Our offices were in the administration building, situated so that we could see the cars pull up to the entrance to admit the child. Occasionally, case material was sent to us before admission, allowing us to make some preliminary judgments about a suitable cottage placement. More often than not, the case material accompanied the child on admission, and we had to make some quick decisions about cottage placement. We took cottage placement seriously because being in a "high grade" or "middle grade" or "low grade" cottage was a difference that made a difference. We could, of course, later change a placement, but that could bring in its wake complications for child and staff.

It was an admission day. A car pulled up and from the back seat emerged a rather large man carrying cradlelike in his arms what from our windows looked like an unusually large child of three or four years of age. But we knew that it could not be a child that young because at that time children had to be at least six years of age to be admitted. We went to the front door of the building to greet the party and only then could we see that what we had thought was a young child was in a fact a much older male. The accompanying material (quite sparse) indicated that he was thirty years of age and had been taken care of from birth by his mother, who had recently died. The father had died years before. Why was he being carried like a baby? He was as gnarled and contorted, as muscularly and neurologically involved, as any case of cerebral palsy I had ever seen—and Southbury had loads of such cases. His body was constantly moving; he was almost constantly drooling; whenever he attempted what seemed to be a purposeful movement, the diffuseness of his body movement became more intense and widespread; and his disfigured face had a wild, "monster-like" quality to it. I looked at this man with puzzlement because I could not understand why he had not been institutionalized earlier. What little material was in the folder that accompanied him indicated that the mother had been opposed to institutionalization. If I was puzzled about that, I was not puzzled about the cottage in which he should be placed: a large, middle-grade cottage that, in truth, had as many low- as middle-grade individuals. Basically, it was a custodial cottage, unrelated to the institution's educational program. Mr. Humphrey (that was his name) was no candidate for an educational program. Of that I was sure!

It was our practice to do a formal psychological assessment within a few days after admission in order to make a final judgment about cottage placement, suitability for programs in the academic school, work assignment, special needs and cautions, etc. In the case of Mr. Humphrey, there was no need, I decided, to do an early assessment. Indeed, I was relieved that there was no particular point to a psychologic assessment in this instance. Those days were quite busy—the opening of Southbury's doors stimulated a stream of admissions (including children from schools that closed their special classes so that their occupants could be sent to Southbury where they became legal and financial wards of the state). Three weeks later, I was walking past the cottage in which Mr. Humphrey had been placed, and Mr. Rooney, the cottage "father" (there was no "mother" in *that* cottage) came out. Mr. Rooney was one of my favorite people and we began to talk about this and that and the state of the world. I remembered that we had not done an assessment of Mr. Humphrey, and I asked Mr. Rooney how he was doing. Mr. Rooney replied: "Now *there* is a smart person. He can read and he understands everything." I was surprised and my face must have shown it because Mr. Rooney, no shrinking violet and a rather good "natural" clinician, invited me to a demonstration of Mr. Humphrey's abilities. Inside the cottage, Mr. Humphrey was lying on the seat of a wheelchair; i.e., he was lying on the seat as if it were a bed. Mr. Rooney left us for a moment and soon returned with a checkerboard in each square of which was a letter of the alphabet, i.e., the top first square had a large *A*, the second a *B*, and so forth. The checkerboard had been one of the things accompanying Mr. Humphrey to Southbury. "Now," Mr. Rooney said, "you ask him a question that requires a one-word answer, then move your finger slowly from one letter to the next and when you have reached the first letter in the answer he will let you know, and you do that for each letter in the answer." How could he let me know if he was in constant motion and if his attempts at vocalization were unintelligible and only increased the level of diffuse bodily activity? I cannot remember what question I put to him, but I do remember that when my finger reached the square containing the first letter of the answer, immediately it was obvious that that was part of the answer—his facial and bodily responses were like a pinball machine gone berserk. He did know the answer to that first question and to almost all of the subsequent ones. I was dumbfounded and I felt stupid, guilty, and quite humble.

I shall not dwell on my diagnostic mistake, which is as unforgivable as it is understandable. I should have known not to go by appearances, or by what a person cannot do, but rather by what a person can learn to do, i.e., by signs of potential assets rather than by exclusive reliance on deficits. I had reacted to Mr. Humphrey as if he were a thing, not a person. Instead of arousing my curiosity, challenging me to figure out how I might relate to this individual, forcing me to keep separate what I was assuming from what was factual, Mr. Humphrey's appearance short-circuited the relationship between what I ordinarily believed and practiced. To someone like me, for whom Itard was a major figure in the pantheon of gods, my response to Mr. Humphrey was, to indulge understatement, quite humbling.

Once I was able to overcome (in part at least) my feelings of stupidity, guilt, and inconsistency, I realized that there were questions far more important than my diagnostic acumen. How did the mother manage to accomplish what she did? What kept her going? What did she recognize in the infant as sparks that could ignite the fires that power learning? What was her theory and in what relation did this stand to her practices? What could we have learned had we had the opportunity to follow and study Mrs. Humphrey in the rearing of her son?

CASE 2

A colleague called to ask if I would, for purposes of assessment, visit a retarded five-year-old boy in a residential nursery in another state. The boy's grandfather, a friend of my colleague, requested an evaluation because the nursery felt that the boy, Andrew, should be moved to another setting. I was reluctant to make the trip and told my colleague that I would prefer seeing the boy in New Haven. This, it turned out, was not possible. The boy's parents had been divorced two or three years earlier, and the father had never visited the nursery; the mother, who lived hundreds of miles away, visited once or twice a year during her shopping expeditions to New York; and the grandfather, who footed all of the boy's bills including my fee, had never visited the boy in the nursery. The grandfather had arranged for a pediatrician in the local community to be available to Andrew. Again reluctantly, I agreed to visit.

I arranged to meet with the pediatrician before going to the nursery. He told me that Andrew had had a mild polio attack from which he had recovered; there was some nonspecific brain damage associated with a "sugar-loaf"-shaped skull and with an awkward gait and other motor movements. Andrew was a nice, likable, obviously retarded child.

The nursery was a large ranch house in a residential neighborhood. I rang the bell, and the door was soon opened by a young boy who, from the pediatrician's description, had to be Andrew. He did have a markedly pointy skull and seemed both distracted and anxious. He said something that was hard for me to comprehend because his articulation was not clear, and he ran back into the house and quickly returned with the chief nurse. The nurse and I talked for a while in one corner of a large living room. Andrew was almost always in sight, not because he was asked to be but, it seemed, because he did not want to be far from the nurse. She told me that Andrew was the only ambulatory child in the nursery, all the others being bed patients. She, it turned out, was the one prodding the grandfather to move the boy to a more socially appropriate and intellectually stimulating environment. She obviously liked Andrew and would miss him terribly, but she could not justify his continued residence there. In fact, she asserted, it had become harmful to his development because there literally was no one there, aside from her, with whom he could have a relationship. After indicating that from time to time she had taken Andrew for a visit to her apartment (she was unmarried), she related an incident from several months earlier. She had to go to the local drugstore for supplies and, for the first time, took Andrew with her. She had started to go into the drugstore when she became aware that Andrew was not at her side. She looked back and there was Andrew, paralyzed by fright and unable to take a step forward or backward.

Instantly she realized that Andrew had never been in a store and was fearful of what awaited there. Aside from the handful of times he had been in her apartment, Andrew had not been out of the nursery and its immediate environs. She took him by the hand, went back to the car, and returned to the nursery. That incident was crucial in leading her to contact the grandfather to convince him to consider placing Andrew elsewhere.

Prior to testing, I tried to interact with Andrew. For one thing, I had trouble making out what he said. No less interfering was his clear reluctance about interacting with me. It seemed to be a reluctance powered by anxiety, which at the time mystified me, although the thought did occur to me that Andrew did not view my visit as being in his best interests. There was something very likable and pathetic about him. As soon as I tried to administer some intelligence test items, his anxiety noticeably increased and, in the most indirect ways, he let me know that he wanted no part of what was going on. It was as if he sensed that I was somebody who could be harmful to him. He whimpered, became tearful, and once or twice got up from his chair to depart. I stopped my efforts at formal testing. I had already concluded that Andrew was markedly retarded, although I did not know how seriously. I had also concluded that, regardless of the degree of retardation, this nursery placement had become dramatically counterproductive and that he had to be placed elsewhere. Finally, and crucially, what concerned me most was the implications of the fact that Andrew had one and only one significant relationship with another human being: the nurse. Psychologically, she was his mother. That is the way he related to her and she felt about him. Theirs was not a nurse-child relationship. I related all of this in a report to the grandfather and urged that it was essential that the nurse accompany Andrew to the new setting and stay with him until he had made some kind of positive adjustment. The thought that Andrew would be picked up at the nursery and taken (psychologically alone) to a new setting interfered with my sleep! I received no reply from the grandfather.

A year or so later, my colleague called me up to say that the grandfather was requesting another evaluation. The nurse, my colleague related, had been persuaded by the grandfather to give up her job and to devote her time and energies to caring for Andrew. He had been placed in a kindergarten in a public school and the immediate question was: Should he be promoted to the first grade, which the school recommended?

I did not need to be urged to visit the nurse and Andrew. Obviously, somebody was selling somebody else a bill of goods! What fool or knave was recommending that the Andrew I had seen a year or so earlier was ready for first grade? The nurse had moved into a garden apartment development. When I steered my car into the development, I had to go at about one mile an hour because the area seemed to consist of more children than blades of grass. I parked the car very near their apartment and, as soon as I got out of the car, a young boy approached. It was Andrew, but what a different Andrew! There was that pointy skull, his motor movements were not graceful but they were far more smooth than when I had first seen him, he spoke with a clarity that amazed me, and he seemed to know and to be on very good terms with the other children. He guided me to the apartment, chitchatting with me. However, even in those early moments, I sensed that he was very ambivalent about my visit, as if he wanted to be his usual giving self but was suspicious about what my agenda was. This became more noticeable later when I tried to test him and, again, I stopped because it seemed upsetting to him. We did enough, though, with my observations, for me to conclude that Andrew tested within the normal range. Whereas on my first visit there was a question about how seriously retarded he was, the question now in my mind was how bright he might be. If on my first visit I intuited a mother-child relationship, I did not have to resort to intuition on my second visit a year or so later. She was a mother constantly seeking ways to stimulate the boy and to help him overcome a pervasive anxiety and self-deprecatory tendency. She told me that within a year or so she would like to move south and take Andrew with her. What did I think? I, of course, said that Andrew should go where she goes. As for promotion to the first grade: of course. Two years later I received a call from the nurse. She and Andrew had moved south and they were both happy and doing well. The reason for the call was that Andrew's mother had visited a number of times in the past year, developed a real interest in the "new" Andrew, and now wanted him to come live with her. How should the nurse respond? I was explicit in recommending that she try to avoid such a change. I also wrote that to the grandfather.

I shall assume that no reader will accuse me of stating or implying that parental love, devotion, and energy are unmixed blessings and that, if these characteristics could be appropriately channeled, scads of retarded persons would become "unretarded." Nor did I wish anyone to conclude that parents possess knowledge and wisdom that professionals do not, as if parents possess a productive interpersonal sensitivity and "natural" clinical acumen that is in short supply among professionals. These are arguable issues, but they are irrelevant to the reasons I have presented these cases.

So what do these cases have to do with charter schools, vouchers, and other reform efforts? The short answer is that they pose the question: What do we mean by learning? Especially if we are educators, the word *learning* is one we use countless times and, yet, if asked to define it, we have no ready answer; we ponder and think (just as we would if we were asked to define *personality, neurosis, thinking,* and similar concepts). Some would say that learning is a process in which some kind and degree of change occurs between what a person knows and has been and what he knows and is at the end of the process. A change observable and measurable has taken place. Some would agree that change is a crucial aspect of the process but would add that the degree of change (or the lack of it) is not explainable without invoking the role of motivation, attitudes, cognitive abilities, personal history. When I have queried educators about their conception of learning, very few of them spontaneously said that an important variable is the adult who plays a crucial role in the process: his or her style, clarity and quality of her pedagogy, way of relating to the students, and more; in brief, the teacher is a fateful, omnipresent variable in how and with what consequences the student experiences learning. Psychologically speaking, the teacher and student are in each other's phenomenology, inevitably so. They are discrete individuals who are "in" each other, each is a part of the other's experience. And, of course, a classroom consists of more than one student, a brute fact of classroom life of which the teacher and each student are quite aware.

What the above forces on us is the realization that learning *always* takes place in a complicated context which has features and purposes shaped by history and tradition: there is one teacher and many students, a predetermined curriculum which is expected to be "learned" in a set period of time determined not by the teacher or students but by policy makers who have no personal relationship with students or teachers. That puts constraints on how teachers think and practice and, therefore, influences how students experience learning. So, when we seek to understand to what degree students do or do not learn, we cannot ignore the ways in which context shapes teachers and students for good or for bad. My preferred way of putting it is in the form of a question: *What are the distinguishing features of contexts of productive and unproductive learning?* And it was that question which recalled to me the cases of Mr. Humphrey and Andy. Let me elaborate on that.

How did Mr. Humphrey's parents get their cerebral-palsied, quadriplegic, ever-in-motion infant to learn what he did? Why did they not, as most parents would have done, however reluctantly, place that infant in an "appropriate" institution? We do not know but the results are so amazing and so unpredicted that we are entitled to indulge speculation. For one thing, they were not taken in by appearances or by what they were told by medical experts of the time. Second, we can assume that they were ever alert to any indication that the child was responsive to this or that effort to make "contact." And if their efforts were many and diverse they were alert to which effort elicited a response and gave direction to subsequent actions. The word *elicited* should not obscure the fact that the child was emitting signals *he* was eliciting *from their* responsiveness. The parents were experimenters searching, interpreting, and reacting to the child's behavior. They found ways to "read" his behavior and each productive reading increased the motivation both of the child and the parents. I am describing features of a context of productive learning for both child and parent. *The parents and child were both learners of and teachers of each other.* Productive learning is never unidirectional.

What would have been a context of unproductive learning? Up until the time Mr. Humphrey was institutionalized he had not experienced a context of unproductive learning. I have observed many similar cases—none as physically and neurologically handicapped as his—who early in their lives were placed in institutions which were contexts of unproductive learning, the kinds of contexts which deservedly came to be regarded as warehouses, which is why those institutions began to be phased out of existence.

What I have speculated to have been the case with Mr. Humphrey was indisputably the case with Andy, who had been placed in the nursery when he was three years of age and where he was the only child who was ambulatory. It took the nurse a while to recognize that this likeable and presumably very retarded child might not be as hopeless as she had been led to believe. She became his mother, so to speak, and played to his assets as she discerned them. They loved each other but that did not prevent her from telling the grandfather that Andy was not in a context where he could learn and grow. As I indicated, she was given the opportunity to create a context of productive learning and she certainly exploited it.

With all of the above as prologue I ask the reader to ponder the following statements, all of which have been substantiated in research.

1. In the modal American classroom (say in a fifty-minute social studies period) the average number of questions asked by students is two. In some classrooms the two questions may be asked by one student. The average number of questions teachers ask varies from forty to well over a hundred.

2. As students go from elementary to middle to high school their regard for and interest in learning steadily decreases, a finding no less true in suburban than in urban schools.

3. As a group teachers consider their preparation for teaching to be very inadequate in preparing them for the realities of classrooms and schools.

4. Teachers are retiring in droves as soon as they become eligible to retire. The number of teachers who leave teaching after their first two or three years of teaching is high and escalating. For the first time ever the number of schools who cannot find people to apply for openings for principals steadily grows.

5. Burnout is the single most frequent reason for the above. If the retirement age for teachers were reduced, the number who would retire would be dramatically higher than it is. Burnout begins well before retirement age. If the eagerness and passion children have when they start school is mightily lessened by the time they finish, it is also the case that the commitment and enthusiasm teachers have when they begin teaching diminishes as the years go on.

The modal American classroom is not a context of productive learning. They are unstimulating, uninteresting places for students who may learn what they are *required* to learn at the expense of any sense of that learning having personal meanings and significances that increase the strength of *wanting* to learn.

How would the reader answer this question: When your child is graduated from high school, what is the one characteristic you want your child to display? There is more than one characteristic you want your child to possess, but is there one that, educationally and intellectually, is the most important? It is by no means easy, I have found, for people to answer the question. But when I give them my answer a large percentage have agreed with me. My answer is that when my child graduates high school I would hope that she would want to continue to learn more about self, others, and the world, to have that passion and curiosity for learning that she had when she started school. By that criterion, far too many schools are contexts which extinguish or lessen passion and curiosity for learning. Please note that the combination of "self, others, and the world" is a way of saying that subject matter is too important, and indeed crucial, to be acquired practically unrelated to personal meanings and interests. That is one of the reasons I presented the two cases. The context of learning prevented that unrelatedness; the two children passionately *wanted* to learn. It is precisely because they are such unusually dramatic cases that they illustrate so starkly the features of a context of productive learning.

What I have just said was said over a hundred years ago by William James in his *Talks to Teachers* (1902) and whose literary style and imagery are far more compelling than mine. Please let us listen to him.

> The negative interests of children lie altogether in the sphere of sensation. Novel things to look at or novel sounds to hear, especially when they involve the spectacle of action of a violent sort, will always divert the attention from abstract conceptions of objects verbally taken in. The grimace that Johnny is making, the spitballs that Tommy is ready to throw, the dog-fight in the street or the distant firebells ringing,—these are the rivals with which the teacher's powers of being interesting have incessantly to cope. The child will always attend more to what a teacher

does than to what the same teacher says. During the performance of experiments or while the teacher is drawing on the blackboard, the children are tranquil and absorbed. I have seen a roomful of college students suddenly become perfectly still, to look at their professor of physics tie a piece of string around a stick which he was going to use in an experiment, but immediately grow restless when he began to explain the experiment. A lady told me that one day, during a lesson, she was delighted at having captured so completely the attention of one of her young charges. He did not remove his eyes from her face; but he said to her after the lesson was over, "I looked at you all the time, and your upper jaw did not move once!" That was the only fact that he had taken in.

Living things, then, moving things, or things that savor of danger or of blood, that have a dramatic quality,—these are the objects natively interesting to childhood, to the exclusion of almost everything else; and the teacher of young children, until more artificial interests have grown up, will keep in touch with her pupils by constant appeal to such matters as these. Instruction must be carried on objectively, experimentally, anecdotally. The blackboard-drawing and story-telling must constantly come in. But of course these methods cover only the first steps, and carry one but a little way.

Can we now formulate any general principle by which the later and more artificial interests connect themselves with these early ones that the child brings with him to the school?

Fortunately, we can: there is a very simple law that relates the acquired and the native interests with each other.

Any object not interesting in itself may become interesting through becoming associated with an object in which an interest already exists. The two associated objects grow, as it were, together: the interesting portion sheds its quality over the whole; and thus things not interesting in their own right borrow an interest which becomes as real and as strong as that of any natively interesting thing. The odd circumstance is that the borrowing does not impoverish the source, the objects taken together being more interesting, perhaps, than the originally interesting portion was by itself.

This is one of the most striking proofs of the range of application of the principle of association of ideas in psychology. An idea will infect another with its own emotional interest when they have become both associated together into any sort of a mental total. As there is no limit to the various associations into which an interesting idea may enter, one sees in how many ways an interest may be derived.

You will understand this abstract statement easily if I take the most frequent of concrete examples,—the interest which things borrow from their connection with our own personal welfare. The most natively interesting object to a man is his own personal self and its fortunes. We accordingly see that the moment a thing becomes connected with the fortunes of the self, it forthwith becomes an interesting thing. Lend the child his books, pencils, and other apparatus: then give them to him, make them his own, and notice the new light with which they instantly shine in his eyes. He takes a new kind of care of them altogether. In mature life, all the drudgery of a man's business or profession, intolerable in itself, is shot through with engrossing significance because he knows it to be associated with his personal fortunes. What more deadly uninteresting object can there be than a railroad timetable? Yet where will you find a more interesting object if you are going on a journey, and by its means can find your train? At such times the timetable will absorb a man's entire attention, its interest being borrowed solely from its relation to his personal life. *From all these facts there emerges a very simple abstract programme for the teacher to follow in keeping the attention of the child: Begin with the line of his native interests, and offer him objects that have some immediate connection with these.* The kindergarten methods, the object-teaching routine, the blackboard and manual-training work,—all recognize this feature. Schools in which these methods preponderate are schools where discipline is easy, and where the voice of the master claiming order and attention in threatening tones need never be heard.

Next, step by step, connect with these first objects and experiences the later objects and ideas which you wish to instill. Associate the new with the old in some natural and telling way, so that the interest, being shed along from point to point, finally suffuses the entire system of objects of thought.

This is the abstract statement; and, abstractly, nothing can be easier to understand. It is in the fulfillment of the rule that the difficulty lies; for the difference between an interesting and a tedious teacher consists in little more than the inventiveness by which the one is able to mediate these associations and connections, and in the dullness in discovering such transitions which the other shows. One teacher's mind will fairly coruscate with points of connection between the new lesson and the circumstances of the children's other experience. Anecdotes and reminiscences will abound in her talk; and the shuttle of interest will shoot backward and forward, weaving the new and the old together in a lively and entertaining way. Another teacher has no such inventive fertility, and his lesson will always be a dead and heavy thing. This is the psychological meaning of the Herbartian principle of "preparation" for each lesson, and of correlating the new with the old. It is the psychological meaning of that whole method of concentration in studies of which you have been recently hearing so much. When the geography and English and history and arithmetic simultaneously make cross-references to one another, you get an interesting set of processes all along the line.

If, then, you wish to insure the interest of your pupils, there is only one way to do it; and that is to make certain that they have something in their minds *to attend with*, when you begin to talk. That something can consist in nothing but a previous lot of ideas already interesting in themselves, and of such a nature that the incoming novel objects which you present can dovetail into them and form with them some kind of a logically associated or systematic whole. Fortunately, almost any kind of a connection is sufficient to carry the interest along (p. 92).

There is a world of difference between exclusively using words to describe a context of productive learning and seeing such a context in action. That is why I urge the reader to see the movie or video *Mr. Holland's Opus.* It doesn't say it all, it *shows* it all. Mr. Holland, no youngster, is a musician-composer who for economic and family reasons "becomes" a teacher, presumably after being "credentialed." Steeped in the traditions and values of classical music, Mr. Holland sees his role as instilling in his audience of high school students an appreciation of "good" music. Whether his audience of students had a knowledge of or interest in such music was not something to which he gave any thought. His role, to him a glimpse of the obvious, was to instill in his audience an appreciation of such music, and by appreciation he meant it in its dictionary sense: to *increase* or enlarge in personal value, certainly not to remain the same or depreciate. When Mr. Holland sees that his audience is unresponsive to his teachings, he does not ask himself why, but he becomes more hortatory and resentful. But the students sit there passively with looks of contempt on their faces. It is a disaster, to the point where he seeks help from others (a friendly teacher, the principal). They are not helpful. Indeed, the friendly teacher reinforces Mr. Holland's opinion that high school students want coddling and entertainment, not a struggle with learning. One day, as a result of a one-on-one interaction with a dispirited, unmusical student, Mr. Holland has an "aha" experience: It hits him with hurricane force that he had never had an inkling of what this girl thought and felt. *Now* he understood her, *now* he knew her. The rest of the film shows how this epiphany causes him radically to redefine his role, methods, and acting style, with the result that the students became alive, interested, and productive. The first half of the film depicts a context of unproductive learning, the second half a context of productive learning. In the first half he is a hapless, ineffective, sleep-producing performer; in the second half his performance is at the Oscar level.

Mr. Holland was prepared to teach the way I am prepared to go to the moon. The movie does not tell us how over the years he had obtained credentials to devote a career to music and musical composition. Nor does the film tell us on what basis he was credentialed to be a teacher, but whatever the basis it was irresponsibly inadequate. That he knew his subject matter is incontestable. That he mightily and desperately strove to "communicate" a subject matter he loved is also incontestable. That he had not the foggiest notion of how to understand students so that he would know where and how to start with them is also incontestable. He acted like some parents do when one day they decide that their child needs to be toilet trained. They promptly begin to "teach" the child in a serious, no-nonsense way, get puzzled when after a week or two the child shows no interest in improvement, they become more serious and pressuring, and on and on in what becomes a battle in a way from which no one escapes psychological injury. You could argue that the comparison is misleading because the two instances are extreme cases. They may be extreme, but they are not infrequent. However, the point of the comparison is that the inadequacies of Mr. Holland's preparation and approach are the norm even though their overt consequences are not as obviously dramatic as in his case. There is good evidence that as students go from elementary to middle to high school their boredom with, dissatisfaction from, and lack of motivation for learning increase. The awe, wonder, curiosity with which children start schooling is, generally speaking, absent or markedly reduced when they are graduated from high school. Over the decades I have observed and talked to and interviewed hundreds of schoolteachers (as well as their students), and it has come as no surprise to me that more formal studies confirmed my personal conclusions and the basic point *Mr. Holland's Opus* illustrates. Teachers, again generally speaking, perform in a way and on a basis that turns off their audiences. In the theater the actor, despite immersion in and identification with a particular role, is acutely sensitive to audience reaction, to any sign that the audience finds his or her portrayal convincing in the intended way. And after opening night the actor waits anxiously for the next day when the newspaper critics will pass judgment on the play and its performers. Some plays close very quickly; there is no opportunity to try to learn from the failure. It is different with the classroom teacher who has the same audience each day. The teacher does not worry about whether the audience will return. The audience, by law and parental authority, must return. The teacher has the opportunity to change her way of interpreting her role depending on how she perceives and interprets audience reaction. Mr. Holland did not interpret them and concluded that the problem was in the minds of the audience; *they* did not understand and appreciate *him*. That it was the other way around could not occur to him, nothing in his preparation alerted him to the fact that his role obligated him to perform in a way to make it believable to students that he was sincerely interested in their thoughts, feelings, reactions, suggestions. It was only after repeated failure and frustration, after he was, so to speak, hit over the head, that he saw his audience in a new light, a light for which he had never been prepared.

I made it my business to ask every educator I met who had seen the movie how he or she felt about it. I probably asked upward of fifty people. Although a few said Mr. Holland was an extreme but not rare case, everyone said that the basic point of the film was valid. And at least half of them spontaneously went on to say that preparatory programs for teachers were blatantly deficient in helping teachers to understand and to devise means for understanding students other than in superficial ways. That critical assessment has been made by teachers ever since formal preparatory programs came into existence as a legally sanctioned way to "professionalize" teaching, to be no more than an agency to credential those seeking such a career.

Not until we gain clarity and agreement about the differences between contexts of productive and unproductive learning will educational reform cease to disappoint us. Vouchers and charter schools, like all other reform efforts, have as their goal improvement in the level and quality of the cognitive development of students, not just the regurgitation of subject matter most of which then ends up in the "file and forget" category. That is certainly a justification proponents of charter schools do not deny. And that is also the case for vouchers which are intended to make it possible for parents to place their children in schools where they will be more challenged and stimulated to exploit their capacities and interests to a degree not considered possible in their present school. In other words, the students go from a context of unproductive learning to a productive one. But on what basis will we be able to make a judgment about their outcomes? The conventional tests we now employ tell us *nothing* about interest, curiosity, creativity, motivation, and learning style. And to my knowledge no one is developing means of conceptualizing and measuring contexts. So we will end up where we began: with personal opinion. That is why in earlier pages I said research was necessary to develop as reliable means as is possible to begin to understand why this classroom or school was successful and other classrooms and schools were not. But that is an old story in the history of educational reforms and it is very likely (in my opinion) that charter schools and vouchers will add new chapters to the story. And that opinion is being offered by someone who in principle is sympathetic to and understanding of why these two movements were predictable reactions to the inadequacies of so many of our schools.

POSTSCRIPT

After this book was finished and being prepared to send to the publishers, the debate in Congress about an educational reform bill began. There are a Senate bill and a House bill which differ in several important ways and it is unclear how those differences will be resolved in a small conference committee of representatives from both bodies. It is beyond my purpose to discuss the two versions in any detail; their similarities are more relevant to my purposes than their differences. Stated most succinctly, the two bills are as clear examples of the shape up or ship out approach to reform as has ever been directed to the public schools. A timetable is laid out whereby yearly the test performance of students will be obtained and made public, failing schools will be identified, and at the end of five years those schools which show no improvement can be disbanded, their students put in other public schools, or privatized, or their funds expended for a voucher program which, in light of the available funds, could only be used by a minuscule number of students.

Question: How are school personnel, especially those in urban areas, likely to interpret and react to the legislation? Will it increase their anxieties, forebodings, and sense of pressure? Will it deepen their resentments because the implicit diagnosis undergirding the legislation is that the inadequacies of schools are caused by school personnel, another instance of unwarranted scapegoating of school personnel, an example of Mencken's caveat that for every major social problem there is a simple answer that is wrong? Is this another example of blaming the victim?

It does not put you into the category of carping critic or gloomer and doomer to predict that school personnel will not embrace the legislation with shouts of glee and relief. *Fear as an incentive for changing and learning has an abysmal track record in child rearing and classroom teaching, as well as in many other types of human relationships where power is unequal.* Anyone familiar with my writings will know that I have been very critical of the inadequacies of school personnel. But they will also know that I put those inadequacies in a context that goes beyond the encapsulated classroom in encapsulated schools, for example, how teachers are selected and trained for the culture and realities of schools. Teachers are no less victims of those factors than are the students they teach. That is why in 1965 I predicted orally and in print that educational outcomes in our schools would on average go downhill. I was 100 percent correct which is why my 1990 book was titled *The Predictable Failure of Educational Reform.* And I now predict that the legislation which will be passed this year in the Congress will again prove my point. What I have said here as in the past was not said cavalierly. If you do not agree with what I have said and predicted, you should feel obliged to familiarize yourself with the history of reform in the post-World War II era with one question in mind: Why is it that one part of the educational system—it is a system of parts, not only schools—has changed the least? I refer, of course, to programs for the selection and preparation of educators. Absent a radical transformation of those programs, we end up proving that the more things change, the more they remain the same. These programs have changed by addition: requiring more of what has been unproductive in the past.

What are *possible* consequences of the new legislation for charter schools and vouchers? Let us start with the following "obituary" circulated by the California Alliance for Public Schools.

OBITUARIES

VOUCHERS, SCHOOL

School vouchers. Passed away on Capital Hill June 12, 2001. Born in 1956 to Milton Friedman, noted libertarian. Defeated by voters more than ten times in the United States. Most recently, suffered overwhelming defeats at the hands of voters in California and Michigan despite generous financial support from wealthy donors. After the election of voucher supporter George W. Bush in 2000, relocated to Washington, D.C. Expected to find greener pastures on Capitol Hill with the support of Bush. Ultimately, however, the popular sentiment against vouchers prevented even Bush from saving vouchers. Defeats in numerous elections, opposition from a broad and diverse coalition of Americans, and voluminous polls, studies, and other research left vouchers in critical condition. Died with a handful of fervent but out-of-the-mainstream supporters on hand. Survived by several elements of the Bush tax plan which aim to sneak a new style of education through privatization through the back door to replace the deceased. Voucher advocates refuse to accept the death of vouchers, spending millions on advertisements, holding pro-voucher conferences, publishing papers and "studies" and meeting with the President to devise schemes to push voucher-like programs. No memorial services are planned.

(Vouchers obituary provided courtesy of the California Alliance for Public Schools, a coalition of community organizations whose mission is to protect and promote public schools.)

Question: What if five years from now it is apparent that the legislation did not have the degree of impact that was its goal? What will the state and federal policy makers conclude? Let us bear in mind that at the end of five years we will also have, we hope, a basis for judging the degree of success of charter schools. What if, as I predict, we will be unable to present a convincing case for robust outcomes? Far more likely is the possibility that their "data" will be murky and uninterpretable. After all, the legislation for either reform does not include funds to carry out a serious evaluation. Both are funded, so to speak, by bottomless hope and prayer, not by a willingness to do it in a way which would allow us to learn by our mistakes. If my prediction is confirmed, to a significant degree at least, I further predict that vouchers and privatization will find a far more accepting audience than they now do.

In my 1993 book, *The Case for Change: Rethinking the Preparation of Educators*, there is a chapter on American medicine in the twentieth century. It may come as a surprise to the reader to learn that early in that century the quality of medical practice and the training of physicians were far worse than the quality of classroom practice and the training of educators today. One of the two most eminent educators of the day was asked to survey all medical schools in the United States and Canada. His name was Abraham Flexner. His report, published critically in 1910, stimulated a truly revolutionary transformation of medical education, which accounts for the subsequent accomplishments in that field. Who commissioned that report? The Carnegie Foundation for the Improvement of *Teaching*. Flexner was not a physician but he knew—when you read his firsthand observations of medical student selection and training you will be aghast—that improvement and advances in any field depend on how it selects and trains its practitioners. It will take more than an Abraham Flexner to start a similar transformation in education today. The problem is horribly complex, the weight of tradition is stifling, and there are many powerful vested interests whose oxen will be gored by a transformation. It will require the opposite of the quick-fix mentality. I confess that I do not have ready answers. But I am secure in the belief that I know what the basic problem is. There are other important problems and they are interrelated but in some ultimate sense the one I have discussed here is bedrock. The California

Alliance for Public Schools wrote an obituary for vouchers, leaving no one in doubt that it expects them to be reincarnated in the not too distant future. The problem I have identified has yet to be born, by which I mean that pitifully few people can see it as deserving to be nurtured and developed, kept alive.

I am quite aware that predicting is a risky affair and, yet, as individuals or organized collectivities we base our actions on some kind of assessment of what the future will be like. The process of thinking ahead forces us to envision a future in which our plans will be realized. We do not like to confront the fact that the present is not pregnant with one future but with a variety of futures. And although there is a part of us that knows that history is not bunk, there is another part that ignores history precisely because it may confront us with ideas and knowledge disturbing to our treasured hopes and visions. To learn from the past requires a degree of interest in the past together with a willingness to at least be dispassionate and to be prepared to change your mind and plans, neither of which we do at all well. Treasured hopes and plans are bulwarks against self-scrutiny and examination of why we think and plan as we do. Nowhere is this more true than in the history of educational reform. That is why I end this book with "The Horse Story," put in the mailbox of my late and dear friend, Dr. Emory Cowen, at the University of Rochester.

HORSE STORY

Common advice from knowledgeable horse trainers includes the adage, *"If the horse you're riding dies, get off."* Seems simple enough, yet in the education business we don't always follow that advice. Instead, we often choose from an array of alternatives that includes:

1. Buying a stronger whip.

2. Trying a new bit or bridle.

3. Switching riders.

4. Moving the horse to a new location.

5. Riding the horse for longer periods of time.

6. Saying things like, "This is the way we've always ridden this horse."

7. Appointing a committee to study the horse.

8. Arranging to visit other sites where they ride dead horses efficiently.

9. Increasing the standards for riding dead horses.

10. Creating a test for measuring our riding ability.

11. Comparing how we're riding now with how we did ten or twenty years ago.

12. Complaining about the state of horses these days.

13. Coming up with new styles of riding.

14. Blaming the horse's parents. The problem is often in the breeding.

15. Tightening the cinch.

We rightly assume that concepts like contexts and learning are central to any explanation of any educational outcome, positive or negative. But there is no consensus about what we mean by those concepts, which is why there is not and cannot be agreement about the significances of those outcomes. The one thing about which there is agreement is that an educational outcome is not a consequence of one factor or even a handful of them. The charter school and voucher movements are an implicit recognition that educational outcomes reflect the interplay of context and learning. The hope is that changing the context-learning relationship will result in better outcomes. That, of course, requires us to ask: How will we know how to explain why and where those changes work in ways we desire and why and where they do not work? We know ahead of time that charter schools and voucher programs will vary in terms of outcomes, if only because they have embarked on uncharted seas. How can we capitalize on predictably mixed results knowing as we do that the explanation will not be simple and uncomplicated? And it is the question that in this book I have said the proponents of charter schools and vouchers have not squarely confronted. To say that, however, is to say that they have not confronted a set of knotty issues which for too long we have discussed in egregiously simplistic ways. If I have convinced the readers of this book that educational reform is far more complicated than they thought (or were led to believe) I will be content. I can assure the reader that I am quite aware that I have not cornered the market on truth and wisdom. But I am also quite aware that the history of educational reform has been one in which oversimplification and well-intentioned passion have obscured the complexity of educational reform.

REFERENCES

The starred references are directly noted in the text. The unstarred are for background reading.

* Alexander, J. Oct. 2, 1991. Interview on MacNeil-Lehrer News Hour. PBS TV.

* Cowden, P., and D. Cohen. n.d. "The Federal Reform of Local Schools in the Experimental Schools Program." Unpublished manuscript available from Peter Cowden c/o Transitions, Solutions, Inc., 177 Worcester Road, Route 9W, Wellesley Hills, MA 02181.

* Greenhouse, S. May 4, 2001. "Union signals softer stance on merit pay." New York Times.

* Heckman, P. 1995. *The Courage to Change*. Newbury Park, CA: Corwin.

* James, W. 1902. *Talks to Teachers on Psychology*. New York: Henry Holt.

  Pauly, E. 1991. *The Classroom Crucible: What Really Works*. New York: Basic Books.

* Rothstein, R. May 2, 2001. "New Ingredient in a Voucher Plan." *New York Times*.

* Sarason, S. B. 1972. *The Creation of Settings and the Future Societies*. San Francisco: Jossey-Bass.

———. 1983. *Schooling in America: Scapegoat and Salvation*. New York: Free Press.

* ———. 1990. *The Predictable Failure of Educational Reform.* San Francisco: Jossey-Bass.

———. 1993. *The Case for Change: Rethinking the Preparation of Educators.* San Francisco: Jossey-Bass.

* ———. 1995. *Parent Involvement and the Political Principle.* New York: Teachers College Press.

———. 1996. *Revisiting the Culture of the School and the Problem of Change.* New York: Teachers College Press.

———. 1997. *How Schools Might Be Governed and Why.* New York: Teachers College Press.

* ———. 1998. *Charter Schools: Another Flawed Educational Reform?* New York: Teachers College Press.

———. 1999. *Teaching as a Performing Art.* New York: Teachers College Press.

———. 2001. *American Psychology and Schools: A Critique.* New York: Teachers College Press.

Stanley, J. 1992. *Children of the Dust Bowl.* New York: Crown.

* Weiss, A. R. 1997. *Going It Alone.* Boston: Institute for Responsive Education, Northeastern University.